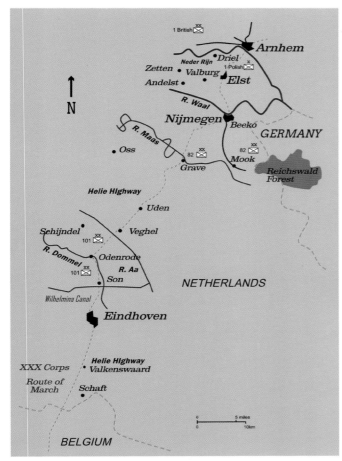

Operation Market Garden would see XXX Corps advance along the Helie Highway (orange dotted line), linking up with 101st (US), 82nd (US) and 1st (UK) Airborne Divisions along the way.

Field Marshal Montgomery examines the remains of a German V-2 rocket near the HQ of Major General Percy Hobart (left), GOC 79th Armoured Division. (IWM)

In the summer of 1944 the Allied campaign in Europe was going well, and it was believed in Supreme Headquarters Allied Expeditionary Force (SHAEF) that the Germans were beaten, with evidence suggesting this was a more than fair assessment. To achieve an effective *coup de grâce* and bring the war to an early close, a plan that was as complex as it was bold was presented by the newly promoted Field Marshal Montgomery.

The operation would also be influenced by several other factors, including the need to secure Dutch ports so that a successful breakthrough into the North German Plain via the

Rhine crossing at Arnhem could be properly supplied. This would also help the current logistical system, which though well supported by the famed 'Red Ball Express', the US-led truck convoy system, was becoming precariously stretched. Then there was also the arrival of the deadly and unpredictable V2 ballistic missile. This counterpart to the V-1 had a speed that gave it a mere five-minute flight from launch in the Netherlands to landing in south-east England. This gave the operation an added impetus and the objective of denying the Germans their V-2 launch sites.

Another equally pressing matter was the growing manpower shortage as a result of losses early in the European campaign which were not being made up as quickly as the Allies hoped. However, there were enough well trained and highly motivated men waiting to be used to help bring the war to an early close in the ranks of the recently formed First Allied Airborne Army. This would be deployed in the largest airborne assault in history with nearly 35,000 men landing in enemy territory, nearly three times the number dropped on D-Day some three months earlier.

Piling on the pressure: American howitzers shell German forces retreating near Carentan, France, 11 July 1944. (NARA)

US paratroopers waiting for the off on the eve of D-Day, 6 June 1944. (NARA)

Highly motivated and well trained: Private Roland Smith, 8th Parachute Battalion, 1st Airborne Division, in defiant pose. (IWM)

Cromwell tanks of the Guards Armoured Division drive along 'Hell's Highway' towards Nijmegen, 20 September 1944. (IWM)

The operation was split into two distinct halves; Market was the airborne element to capture vital bridges as part of *coup de main* operations and Garden was the ground assault which would consolidate the airborne gains and create a sizable salient in enemy territory. However, planning, coordination and intelligence were not as thorough or as abundant as previous operations. This turned Market Garden from a glorious adventure into a devastating defeat for the Allies and the near-destruction of I Airborne Corps.

For the German defenders it would see them stop the rot of headlong retreat and organizational chaos and galvanize an effort to stop the Allied advance. The troops of the SS would face off against a more than equal adversary in the airborne troops, who tested their resolve and fought like the devil himself. Indeed such was their aggressive battlefield spirit that they would live up to their now-familiar nickname of the 'Red Devils'.

Meanwhile the armour of XXX Corps, which two years earlier had chased Panzerarmee Afrika out of Egypt, would find itself slowed by its advance along a single main road, the Helie or 'Hell's' Highway. Combined with effective German defences, including engineering operations, and an ever-lengthening timetable of operations, they would never reach the bridge at Arnhem in time to support and relieve Lieutenant Colonel John Frost's Paras on the ground.

Market Garden would also show a normally cautious Montgomery take an uncharacteristic gamble. As Lieutenant General Sir Frederick Browning, commander of I Airborne Corps, would remark during a planning meeting 'I think we might be going a bridge too far'.

Wearing their iconic maroon berets, paratroopers of 6th Airborne Division, including members of the parachute ambulance units, enjoy a final cigarette with RAF aircrew before boarding their transport. (MOD UK)

Hours from disaster. Taken on 19 September 1944, this aerial view of the bridge over the Neder Rijn, Arnhem shows British troops and destroyed German armoured vehicles visible at the north end of the bridge. (IWM)

OPERATION MARKET GARDEN – A BRIDGE TOO FAR

Operation Market Garden featured well known and notable commanders on all sides, but there are commanders whose quality and influence in the battle marked them above their peers in many respects.

ALLIED COMMANDERS

Bernard Law Montgomery had been originally commissioned in the Royal Warwick Regiment in 1908, though barely as he was expelled for fighting and rowdiness during his studies at the Royal Military College Sandhurst. During the First World War Montgomery was wounded twice and awarded the Distinguished Service Order. Between the wars various command and staff appointments followed, including tours in Palestine and India. As Officer Commanding 9th Infantry Brigade Montgomery arranged an amphibious combined-operations exercise for the new Commander-in-Chief of Southern Command, General Sir Archibald Wavell. This experience would serve Montgomery well in the war years.

In 1939 Montgomery took command of 3rd (Iron) Infantry Division, deploying to Belgium as part of the British Expeditionary Force (BEF). During the 'Phoney War' he pushed his men hard, ensuring training and discipline was maintained. As a result his division had the best performance of any British unit during the Battle of France and subsequent withdrawal of BEF. Montgomery's persistence and high standards had paid dividends. It was during Operation Dynamo that Montgomery assumed command of II Corps from Lieutenant General Sir Alan Brooke.

Montgomery's new fighting spirit. A soldier of the 12th Battalion, Hampshire Regiment, emerges from the smoke. (IWM)

On his return to the UK Montgomery was given the command of V Corps, and busied himself with preparations for the defence of Hampshire and Dorset, where he worked under Auchinleck. The working relationship between the two was far from congenial and the effects continued long after the two parted ways. In 1941 Montgomery took command of XII Corps, based in Kent, this was subsequently extended to cover Sussex and Surrey. He continued to push his troops hard, demanding excellence in terms of physical fitness and

Field Marshal Montgomery with his corps divisional commanders at Walbeck, Germany, 22 March 1945. (IWM)

France 1940: Major General Bernard Montgomery, GOC 3rd Division, Lieutenant General Sir Alan Brooke, GOC II Corps, and Major General Dudley Johnson, GOC 4th Division. (IWM)

capacity. To engender an offensive spirit he renamed his command the South-Eastern Army, holding an impressive combined-forces exercise involving over 100,000 troops in May 1942. During this time he was promoted to lieutenant general.

Arriving in Egypt in July Montgomery got to work training his new charges, making sweeping changes and taking the fight to Panzerarmee Afrika at the Second Battle of El Alamein. Within six months he had pushed the Axis forces to defeat and had his eye on the next prize, Europe.

To Victory! 25pdr field guns and 'Quad' artillery tractors parade past Winston Churchill during his visit to Tripoli, 4 February 1943. Note air recognition roundels on the roofs. (IWM)

British Army jeeps leading a column including universal carriers and a Sexton 25pdr self-propelled gun moving toward Caen, 1 August 1944. (IWM)

He would lead the Eighth Army across the Mediterranean to Sicily and Italy, where his slow and steady pace, in particular along the eastern side of Italy, infuriated his American allies, most notably Patton. By the end of 1943 Montgomery had returned to Great Britain to help plan the upcoming invasion of Northern Europe, Operation Overlord. There he would be given command of Allied ground forces which had been gathered under 21st Army Group and would lead the liberation of Europe. His first test as a general came in the form of the city of Caen. Montgomery was convinced he could take it within days of the landing; however, the city didn't fall until two months after D-Day. This prolonged battle did little for his reputation in the eyes of the Americans, with Patton joined by Omar Bradley in his criticism of Montgomery's skills. However, Montgomery went on to surprise his detractors with the successful defeat of most of Army Group B in the Falaise Pocket. On 1 September 1944 Montgomery was promoted to field marshal in an attempt to alleviate his disappointment at not being Supreme Allied Commander.

Lieutenant General Brian Horrocks was commissioned into the Middlesex Regiment on 8 August 1914, four days after Britain's entry into the First World War. An eventful war saw Horrocks retreat with the BEF at the Battle of Mons. His war was cut short on 21 October at the Battle of Armentières, where he was wounded in the lower abdomen and upper thigh, and was taken prisoner, where his treatment at the hands of his captors was often inhumane. Whilst a prisoner Horrocks made attempts to escape, learned Russian and was regularly moved between camps to prevent further escape attempts.

After the end of the war Horrocks found himself part of the Allied intervention in the Russian Civil War in the spring of 1919 where his diplomatic skills and knowledge of Russian would help defuse many a fraught situation. In January 1920 Horrocks once again found himself a prisoner of war, this time of the Red Army. Released in October Horrocks returned to

the Middlesex Regiment, who were now part of the British Army of the Rhine, before moving on to Ireland and Silesia. In 1924 Horrocks represented Great Britain in the Paris Olympics before going on to fulfil command and instructor postings with both the regular and Territorial Army, which he enjoyed immensely.

When war broke out in 1939 Horrocks was an instructor at the Staff College, Camberley, designing a shorter officer training course. Promoted to lieutenant colonel in December 1939, he was despatched to France to command the 2nd Battalion, Middlesex Regiment in 1940 as part of Montgomery's 3rd Division. Within weeks of his arrival Horrocks's skills led to a temporary promotion to brigadier and command of 11th Brigade. On returning to the UK he assumed command of 9th Brigade and by June 1941 had been promoted to acting major general in command of 44th (Home Counties) Infantry Division.

A new type of warfare. Horrocks taking part in Exercise Limpet in the Thetford–Bury St Edmunds area as GOC of 9th Armoured Division. (IWM)

March 1942 brought another command, this time the recently formed 9th Armoured Division, his acting rank changing to major general in June. As he had no armour experience Horrocks set about training his troops hard so he could grasp the intricacies of armoured warfare. In the summer of 1942 Horrocks was on the move once again and was sent to North Africa to command XIII Corps with the acting rank of lieutenant general where he would take part in the defence of Alam Halfa and the Second Battle of El Alamein.

In December 1942 he took command of X Corps which led the final offensive in North Africa between April and May 1943, accepting the surrender of the remnants of Rommel's Army Group Africa. He was promoted to temporary lieutenant general and war-substantive major general, but in June he would be wounded once more, this time seriously, taking a year to recover.

Desert 'O' Group: Horrocks, along with Brigadier 'Pip' Roberts, commander of the Eighth Army's only surviving Grant tanks, listens to orders from Montgomery. (IWM)

In August 1944, Horrocks assumed command of XXX Corps in France, advancing 400km (250 miles) in only six days and liberating Brussels. Horrocks and XXX Corps would lead the ground assault element of Market Garden and push through the Netherlands and on into the northern Germany.

General Horrocks, as GOC XXX Corps, visiting American troops in Argentan, 21 August 1944. (IWM)

Lieutenant General Frederick Browning was commissioned into the Grenadier Guards in 1915, serving on the Western Front where he won the Distinguished Service Order and the Croix de Guerre. Between the wars Browning served in several posts, including Adjutant of Sandhurst, where he rode his mount into the Grand Entrance of the Old College which started a tradition which continues almost a century later. He also represented Great Britain in the 1928 Winter Olympics in the five-man bobsleigh event. In 1935 Browning was promoted to lieutenant colonel and given command of the 2nd Grenadier Guards before taking command of the Small Arms School in 1939 as a full colonel.

Lieutenant General F.A.M. Browning, training at RAF Netheravon, October 1942. (IWM)

In May 1940 he was promoted to brigadier and given the command of 128th (Hampshire) Infantry Brigade, part of the BEF, until early 1941 when he was given command of the 24th Guards Brigade. By November Browning had been promoted to major general and commander of the 1st Airborne Division. Browning set about designing his new division, both in spirit and appearance, including the Parachute Regiment's famous Bellerophon riding Pegasus tactical flash patch and Army Air Corps pilot's brevet. In 1942, as well as fashioning the *esprit de corps* of Britain's new airborne legions, he also qualified as a pilot and saw first-hand how US airborne forces were developing as a fighting force.

Browning standing by a Douglas Dakota of RAF Transport Command at RAF Lyneham, Wiltshire, after being flown back from Normandy. (IWM)

Brigadier General James Gavin with Browning after the airborne landings in Overasselt. (Regionaal Archief Nijmegen)

By November 1942 elements of Browning's new division had received their baptism of fire in Operation Torch, when the nickname 'Red Devils' was first given to his men, an accolade he relished and propagated among them.

In April 1943, Browning become Airborne Advisor to the Allied Supreme Commander Eisenhower, and oversaw the planning of the airborne assault on Sicily. He was then promoted lieutenant general in December of that year and assigned to HQ Airborne Forces in Britain. The following April, he assumed command of I Airborne Corps, which would become part of Brereton's First Allied Airborne Army, commanded by US Lieutenant General Lewis H. Brereton, in August 1944. At this time Browning also became Deputy Commander of the

Major General Roy Urquhart outside his headquarters of the Hotel Hartenstein before Operation Berlin.

Army. Browning and I Airborne Corps would go on to lead the airborne forces committed during Market Garden.

Major General Roy Urquhart was commissioned into the 1st Battalion, Highland Light Infantry (HLI) on 24 December 1920. Between the wars he followed the same path as many of his contemporaries including a stint at the Staff College, Camberley from 1936 to 1937, thereafter serving with the 2nd Battalion, HLI in the Arab revolt before moving on to India. Urquhart remained in India until 1941 when he was posted to North Africa before being sent back to the United Kingdom, to serve as a staff officer in the 3rd Infantry Division.

He was then promoted to lieutenant colonel commanding 2nd Battalion, Duke of Cornwall's Light Infantry until 1942 when he was appointed as a staff officer in the 51st (Highland) Infantry Division, based in North Africa. He then commanded the 231st Infantry Brigade for the Allied invasion of Sicily and the early stages of the Italian campaign before returning to England where he was placed with XII Corps as a staff officer. In 1944 Urquhart assumed command of the 1st Airborne Division, even though he had no command experience of an airborne formation, going on to lead the division in Market Garden.

Brigadier General James Gavin joined the US Coast Artillery, albeit underage, in 1924. In his spare time Gavin fed his passion for learning and under the mentoring of his sergeant applied to a local army school, from which the best graduates got the chance to attend the United States' Military Academy at West Point, New York. He applied himself thoroughly and passing the necessary examinations was admitted into West Point in 1925.

Numerous postings around the US and in the Philippines followed until a return to West Point in 1940 occurred, allowing him to study German Blitzkrieg tactics whilst undertaking instructor duties. Of great interest was the use of German airborne troops especially the daring assault on Fort Eben-Emael in Belgium in May 1940, where glider-borne troops had captured the fort in a stunning night attack.

Major General James Gavin receiving the DSO from Field Marshal Sir Bernard Montgomery in Mönchengladbach. (HMSO)

Gavin then volunteered for a posting to the new airborne unit in April 1941, where he was accepted and began training at Fort Benning in August 1941. His first command appointment was commanding officer of 'C' Company of the newly established 503rd Parachute Infantry Battalion He was subsequently

Fallschirmjäger from the Koch assault detachment after the battle for Fort Eben-Emael in Belgium, (Bundesarchiv)

A paratrooper at Fort Benning, Georgia, practises the art of grenade throwing. (US Govt)

Train hard, fight easy. Manhandling a 37mm anti-tank gun into position. (US Govt)

promoted to major in October, developing tactics for airborne combat.

In August 1942, Gavin became the commanding officer of the 505th Parachute Infantry Regiment (PIR) at Fort Benning and was promoted to colonel shortly thereafter. Gavin built this regiment, placing great store in leading by example in all things and providing his battalion with realistic training exercises and routines.

In February 1943 the 505th PIR was assigned to the 82nd Airborne Division to assist in Operation Husky, the invasion of Scilly launched from North Africa, where it would make the first ever regimental-sized airborne landing. In December

1943 Gavin was promoted to brigadier general, becoming the assistant divisional commander of the 82nd Airborne as well one of the youngest generals of the war. By spring 1944 the 82nd Airborne were in Great Britain preparing for D-Day.

On D-Day Gavin and the 82nd were split into three forces to secure an area of roughly 26km^2 (10 square miles) around the Merderet River, but due to poor weather the drops were scattered across the French countryside. Whilst problematic for commanders, the scattered drops gave the Germans the impression the number of paratroops was much larger than it actually was, which helped aid the success of the assault. In late summer Gavin assumed command of the 82nd Airborne Division which he would lead into combat in Market Garden.

Waves of American paratroopers land near Grave, Holland, during Operation Market Garden, while livestock graze peacefully near gliders that landed earlier. (US Army)

Operation Husky was not the success the airborne commanders had hoped it would be. Coast Guardsmen listen to a paratrooper explain what happened when his unit dropped on Sicilian soil. (US Coast Guard)

AXIS COMMANDERS

Generalfeldmarschall Walter Model was commissioned into the 52nd Infantry Regiment von Alvensleben in 1910 serving as part of the 5th Division on the Western Front. During the war Model was posted to several units, serving as an adjutant and company commander, as well as completing an abbreviated staff officers' course.

After the war he continued to serve in the Reichswehr in the elite 3rd Infantry Division as well as instructing students undertaking the General Staff training course on tactics and advocating military modernization. By 1938, Model was a Generalmajor, and like many contemporary army officers

supported the Nazi regime. He developed close professional relationships with senior Nazis, including Goebbels and Speer.

Model started the Second World War as the chief of staff of IV Corps during the invasion of Poland, and then the Sixteenth Army during the Battle of France. A promotion to Generalleutnant followed in April 1940, with his first senior command posting in November to the 3rd Panzer Division.

He developed a combined arms training programme where men were thrown together in various ad-hoc groupings regardless of their parent unit, anticipated the later use of Kampfgruppen by the Germans in the Second World War. While this would become routine later on, it was still not universal.

For Operation Barbarossa, the 3rd Panzer Division was part of the XXIV Panzer Corps. Guderian engendered an aggressive

Model (in coat) talking to the crew of a StuG III ausf G assault gun on the Eastern Front. (Wydawnictwo Prasowe Kraków-Warszawa)

Model as GOC 3rd Panzer Division with the commander of the Second Panzer Army, Heinz Guderian, at the start of Operation Barbarossa. (Unknown)

German soldiers take a minute to eat during the retreat from Moscow in 1941. (MoD [Rus. Fed.])

spirit in this division which saw it achieve remarkable advances early in the campaign. With the fall of Smolensk, Model's division turned south towards Kiev forming part of a pincer movement. With the fall of Kiev came another promotion, this time to General der Panzertruppe and command of XLI Panzer Corps, which was entangled in Operation Typhoon, the assault on Moscow. Despite high corps morale, Model was pitted against 'General Winter', poor supplies and a massive Soviet counter-attack. Model was put in charge of managing the retreat, which he prevented from becoming a rout.

Throughout 1942 and 1943 Model's skill at holding the line continued to serve him well and by March 1943 he had been

promoted to Generalfeldmarschall. By 1944 Model was moving between Army Groups in the East, merely slowing Soviet advances, but the situation in Normandy was becoming increasingly perilous. Despite requests for extra men and material, which failed to be supplied, Model did his best to hold the Allied advance. By high summer the tide could not be stopped and Model found himself and his men in a fighting retreat to the German border. Model established his headquarters at Oosterbeek, where he began to rebuild Army Group B as well as taking the temporary mantle of Oberbefehlshaber (Supreme Commander) West. When word of the arrival of the 1st Airborne Division reached Model he was convinced they were coming to capture him and fled his HQ.

General Kurt Student (2nd left) during a conference with soldiers in Crete. Also visible is an officer of the 85th Mountain Rifle Regiment. (Wydawnictwo Prasowe Kraków-Warszawa)

General Friedrich Christiansen (third from the left) arrives in The Hague as Supreme Commander of the German Armed Forces in the Netherlands. He remained in this post for the duration of the Second World War. (Rijksmuseum)

General der Flieger Friedrich Christiansen joined the merchant marine in 1895, serving for seven years before changing career and learned to fly in 1913. With the outbreak of war Christiansen was called up as a naval aviator flying seaplanes over the North Sea, the English Channel and Britain in a number of roles. By the end of the war Christiansen was an ace and had earned the Pour le Mérite and was promoted to Kapitänleutnant.

Between the wars Christiansen returned to the merchant marine before being employed by Dornier as a pilot. His reputation and skills saw him head hunted by the Reichsluftfahrtministerium (RLM – Reich Aviation Ministry), and in 1936 he was promoted to Generalmajor. In April 1937 he was appointed Korpsführer and promoted to Generalleutnant of the Nationalsozialistsches Flieger-Korps (NSFK – National Socialist Flyers Corps). On 1 January 1939 he was promoted once again to General der Flieger. From 29 May 1940 until 7 April 1945 Christiansen was Wehrmachtbefehlshaber in den Niederlanden (Supreme Commander of the Wehrmacht in the Netherlands).

Generaloberst Kurt Student was commissioned a lieutenant in March 1911, qualifying as a pilot in 1913 and serving in the First World War as an ace with the 'Fokker Scourge'. Between the wars Student became involved in military gliders, transferring from the Army to the newly-formed Luftwaffe as head of its training schools. In July 1938, he was named commander of airborne and air-landing troops, and in September commanding general of the 7th Air Division, Germany's first Fallschirmjäger division.

The 7th were first deployed during the invasions of Norway and Denmark including the first large-scale airborne operation in history, the battle for The Hague. During airborne operations in the Battle of Rotterdam, Student was hit in the head by a stray German round. The Fallschirmjäger went on to achieve their most notable success with the assault on Fort Eben-Emael by only eighty-five men. Subsequently Student was awarded the Knight's Cross of the Iron Cross.

In January 1941, Student assumed command of the XI. Fliegerkorps and in May Student directed Unternehmen Merkur (Operation Mercury), the airborne invasion of Crete, which saw huge numbers of paratroopers lose their live. Such was the Fallschirmjägers' sacrifice that Hitler forbade all future major airborne operations, despite Merkur's success.

In 1943, Student ordered Major Harald Mors to plan Unternehmen Eiche (Operation Oak), a combined Fallschirmjäger /SS operation that freed Benito Mussolini. He received the Oak Leaves to the Knight's Cross for his role in the operation. Student was transferred to Italy and later to France, where he was involved in the battles of Normandy in 1944. He was in command of the 1st Fallschirm-Armee at the time of Market Garden.

Situation briefing with (from left) Generalfeldmarschall Walter Model, Generaloberst Kurt Student, Obergruppenführer Wilhelm Bittrich, Major Hans Peter Knaust, and Gruppenführer Heinz Harmel. (Bundesarchiv)

For brevity the ORBAT of all sides has been broken down to corps and divisional, Special Forces and independent Allied brigade level only. The list also shows how large and ambitious Market Garden was. Commanders listed were effective 27 September 1944.

ALLIED FORCES
First Allied Airborne Army – Lieutenant General Lewis H. Brereton, USAAF
XVIII Airborne Corps – Major General Matthew Ridgeway
82nd Airborne Division – Brigadier General James Gavin
101st Airborne Division – Major General Maxwell Taylor

I Airborne Corps – Lieutenant General Frederick Browning
1st Airborne Division – Major General Roy Urquhart
52nd (Lowland) Division (Air Transportable) – Major General Edmund Hakewill-Smith
Polish 1st Independent Parachute Brigade – Major General Stanisław Sosabowski

Air Assets
United States Army Air Forces (USAAF)
IX Troop Carrier Command – Major General Paul Williams
50th Troop Carrier Wing – General Julian M. Chappell
52d Troop Carrier Wing – Brigadier-General Harold Clark
53d Troop Carrier Wing – Brigadier General Maurice Beach

RAF
No. 38 Group RAF – Air Vice Marshal Leslie Hollinghurst
No. 46 Group RAF – Air Commodore Lawrence Darvall

21st Army Group – Field Marshal Bernard Montgomery
British Second Army – Lieutenant General Miles Dempsey
VIII Corps – Lieutenant General Richard O'Connor
11th Armoured Division – Major General George Roberts
3rd Infantry Division – Major General Lashmer Whistler
49th (West Riding) Infantry Division – Lieutenant General Evelyn Barker
1st Belgian Infantry Brigade – Colonel Jean-Baptiste Piron

XII Corps – Lieutenant General Neil Ritchie
7th Armoured Division – Major General Gerald Verney
15th (Scottish) Infantry Division – Major General Colin Barber
53rd (Welsh) Infantry Division – Major General Robert Ross

XXX Corps – Lieutenant General Brian Horrocks
Guards Armoured Division – Major General Allan Adair
43rd (Wessex) Infantry Division – Major General Ivor Thomas
8th Armoured Brigade – Brigadier George Prior-Palmer
Royal Netherlands Brigade 'Prinses Irene' – Colonel Albert de Ruyter van Steveninck

Allied Air Forces
Royal Air Force
Second Tactical Air Force – Air Marshal Sir Arthur Coningham
No. 83 Group RAF – Air Vice-Marshal Harry Broadhurst
No. 2 Group RAF – Air Vice-Marshal Basil Embry
Fighter Command – Air Marshal Roderick Hill
Bomber Command – Air Chief Marshal Sir Arthur Harris
RAF Coastal Command – Air Chief Marshal Sholto Douglas

United States Army Air Forces (USAAF)
US Eighth Air Force – Lieutenant General James Doolittle
US Ninth Air Force – Lieutenant General Hoyt Vandenberg

AXIS FORCES
It must be remembered that at this stage of the war a great many German units were understrength with their command and control structures in tatters, but even so the experience and resources that Model could draw upon remained formidable.

German Armed Forces Group (AFG) Netherlands – General der Flieger Friedrich Christiansen
Seventh Army – General der Panzertruppe Erich Brandenberger
II SS-Panzerkorps – Obergruppenführer Wilhelm Bittrich
9th SS Panzer Division 'Hohenstaufen' – Obersturmbannführer Walther Harzer
10th SS Panzer Division 'Frundsberg' – Gruppenführer Heinz Harmel
Kampfgruppe 'Von Tettau' – Generalleutnant Hans von Tettau

Army Group B – Generalfeldmarschall Walther Model
Fifteenth Army – General der Infanterie Gustav-Adolf von Zangen

LXVII Armeekorps – General Otto M. Hitzfeld
346th Infantry Division – Generalleutnant Erich Diester
711th Static Division – Generalleutnant Josef Reichert
719th Coastal Division – Generalleutnant Karl Sievers

LXXXVIII. Armeekorps – General Hans Reinhard
245th Infantry Division – Oberst Gerhard Kegler
59th Infantry Division – Generalleutnant Walter Poppe
Kampfgruppe 'Chill' – Generalleutnant Kurt Chill

1st Fallschirm-Armee – Generaloberst Kurt Student
II Fallschirm-Korps – General der Fallschirmtruppen Eugen Meindl
3rd Fallschirmjäger Division – Generalmajor Walter Wadehn
5th Fallschirmjäger Division – Generalmajor Sebastian-Ludwig Heilmann

XII SS-Armeekorps SS-Obergruppenführer Curt von Gottberg
180th Infantry Division – Generalmajor Bernhard Klosterkemper
190th Infantry Division – Generalleutnant Ernst Hammer
363rd Volksgrenadier Division – Generalleutnant Augustus Dettling

LXXXVI Corps – General der Infanterie Hans von Obstfelder
Division 'Erdmann' – Generalleutnant Wolfgang Erdmann
176th Infantry Division – Oberst Christian-Johannes Landau

Wehrkreis VI, Corps 'Feldt' – General der Kavallerie Kurt Feldt

Luftwaffe West – Generaloberst Otto Deßloch / Generalleutnant Alexander Holle
IX. Fliegerkorps – Generalmajor Dietrich Peltz
II. Jagdkorps – General Alfred Bülowius
Generalkommando III. Flakkorps – General Wolfgang Pickert

By the beginning of high summer in 1944 the Allies were once again on the move and pushing out of the Normandy bridgehead. They drove all before them, sweeping defending Axis forces mercilessly aside and thanks to total air supremacy were able to prevent commanders on the ground from organizing any meaningful resistance. But for all this the Allied position remained delicate; the further they pushed out of Normandy the longer their supply lines became, and it wasn't until the liberation of Antwerp on 2 September that a deep-water port became available. Still, the problem was that even though the port was in good condition, access via the Scheldt Estuary remained covered by German guns, which presented an unacceptable risk to shipping.

An enthusiastic welcome for the vanguard. A Humber scout car crew are greeted by local people in the town of Gacé in Normandy, 23 August 1944. (IWM)

Feeding the front. Corporal Charles H. Johnson of the 783rd Military Police Battalion waves on a 'Red Ball Express' motor convoy rushing materiel to the front. (NARA)

Until these guns were neutralized the Allies would have to content themselves with being supplied by the famous 'Red Ball Express'. However, it was felt that the speed of the Allied advance, which had overtaken official planning estimates, would quickly isolate the defenders and in time lead to the liberation of Belgium and the Netherlands. Indeed intelligence reports coming from the Dutch Resistance in occupied zones reported multiple German retreats. If true, the Allies would simply advance and roll into Northern Germany relatively unopposed. This was considered viable, especially given the presence of 2.1 million Allied troops and nearly 500,000 vehicles.

The Allies' ORBAT had also firmed up, with armies now holding sway over defined areas of responsibility. By the beginning of September 1944 Montgomery's 21st Army Group, made up of the Canadian First Army and British Second Army, was poised by the Belgian/Dutch border. To its immediate south was the 12th Army Group, consisting of the First and Third US Armies.

Opposing these armies were the shattered and exhausted German forces. Model's Army Group B consisting of the Seventh and Fifteenth Armies and the First Parachute Army faced Montgomery's 21st Army Group. To the south sat Blaskowitz's Army Group G, consisting primarily of the Fifth Panzer Army, positioned behind the German national border.

To bolster these armies were numerous Kampfgruppen, stragglers and isolated units formed into fighting groups led by senior commanders into a coherent force often filled with more than capable veterans, but also with the old, disabled and inexperienced. Commanders on the ground really did have a mixed bag.

Some old, something borrowed, something new: Generalfeldmarschall Erwin Rommel inspecting a Buete Panzer (lit. captured tank), a Renault UE 28-32 cm Wurfrahmen auf Infanterie-Schlepper UE(f) in Normandy, May 1944. For the defence of Northern Europe the Germans employed a great deal of ingenuity. (Bundesarchiv)

Another issue for the Allies that some 60,000 German troops, with a considerable amount of direct and indirect support weaponry, had been evacuated into Holland via the Scheldt Estuary, thus bolstering local defences. Two of these evacuated divisions, the 59th and 245th, were sent to bolster the defences in the Dutch province of Brabant. Their presence would make a big impact on Allied troops as they advanced north and stiff German resistance held up any crossing of the Albert Canal until 8 September.

By this point the British advance in particular had mostly stopped to give logistical support the opportunity to catch up. As a result Model was given some breathing space and quickly set to organizing his forces in the Netherlands into something resembling a cohesive defence. Quickly realizing this, the

By late summer the Germans were losing the numbers game, no matter how experienced their troops were. A dug-in Panzer IV of the 1/22nd Panzer Regiment, photographed near Lebisey after being knocked out during the Battle for Caen. (IWM)

Lieutenant General Miles C. Dempsey (right), seen here with General Montgomery (centre) and General Omar N. Bradley (left), was unimpressed by Montgomery's ambitious plan and raised concerns over its scope. (IWM)

Allies knew they could not afford it and a plan was drawn up to continue the advance. This would see the 21st Army Group swing northward and force a salient into the German lines towards the town of Arnhem, a mere 30 minutes north-west of the German border. This would then become a springboard for an Allied advance into Germany proper, completely bypassing the defences of the Siegfried Line. It would also sever support for the new 'Vengeance Weapon', the V-2, being fired from the area around the Hook of Holland.

Sergeant E. Walter of the Army Film and Photographic Unit (AFPU) examines an artillery piece, a vital piece of equipment, abandoned during the German retreat, 16 July 1944. (IWM)

Montgomery, a commander normally given to caution and careful planning, drew up a plan that was as ambitious as it was reckless. Designated Market Garden the plan would see two major advances, one by land, led by Dempsey's Second Army, which had followed Montgomery since El Alamein and was designated Garden. Their line of advance would follow Highway 69, later referred to as 'Hell's Highway', northwards, crossing and connecting the objectives that were to be taken by the airborne element of the operation, Market.

Market required three divisions of the First Allied Airborne Army to simultaneously drop and take a series of key points. The American 101st Division led by Major General Matthew Ridgway would liberate and take Eindhoven and subsequent river crossings to the north. Brigadier General James Gavin and his troops of the 82nd Division would take the bridges at Grave which crossed the Maas and at Nijmegen which crossed the Waal. Added to this Gavin was further tasked with the capture of the Groesbeek Heights, an area of high ground to the south-east.

General Matthew Ridgway, seen here at Sicily, had helped design the airborne component of Operation Husky and was experienced in glider and paratroop assaults. (US Army)

This left the British 1st Airborne Division, led by Major General Roy Urquhart, to seize the crossing at Arnhem over the Neder Rijn. Meanwhile I Airborne Corps, led by Lieutenant General Frederick Browning, would be deployed to the Nijmegen area of operations and General Stanisław Sosabowski's 1st Polish Parachute Brigade would land near Driel to support operations around Nijmegen.

Of the two plans Market was the most complex. For Garden Dempsey merely had to point his forces north and roll forward 116km (72 miles) into the Netherlands, join the dots between

A Polish paratrooper puts a British SORBO training helmet on the British Deputy Prime Minister Clement Atlee whilst Major General Sosabowski looks on. (Wydawnictwo Prasowe Kraków-Warszawa)

Down, but most certainly not out: In the Netherlands the Germans could draw on experienced troops such as these Fallschirmjäger. Their tenacity in battle would come as a shock to the advancing Allies. (Bundesarchiv)

the airborne forces and handle the occasional piece of military engineering. It was the airborne commanders who had the most dangerous tasks; they had the dubious honour of taking numerous river crossings without armour support, in a region where the intelligence picture was less than sharp. Another issue was the deployment of the airborne forces, which numbered nearly 35,000 men, the largest airborne assault in history; there simply weren't enough aircraft for the job.

To achieve his ambitious goals Montgomery interceded with Eisenhower to not only back his plan, but to also give Market Garden the necessary logistical support, which meant Patton, would have to halt his own advance with his Third Army in the south. Eisenhower, clearly impressed, agreed to Montgomery's plan, with a D-Day of 17 September, though his commanders still had their doubts. Browning, who asked Montgomery how long his troops at Arnhem would be expected to wait for support, was told two days. He responded his troops would be able to hold their ground for four days at the most.

No plan survives first contact with the enemy, and Market Garden would become an excellent example of that age-old adage.

USAAF Douglas C-47A Skytrains from the 88th Troop Carrier Squadron, 438th Troop Carrier Group, 53rd Troop Carrier Wing, 9th Troop Carrier Command, tow Waco CG-4A gliders during the invasion of France in June 1944. (USAF)

This meant that the drop would be spread over three days, with troops going in first, followed by artillery and engineering support as well as reinforcements on the second day and further reinforcements on the third day. A further complication was locating suitable landing zones, especially for the glider force. Such was the lack of suitable landing sites that the I Airborne Corps would land 10km (6 miles) from the Rhine bridge in Arnhem. Another concern, especially from seasoned commanders like Sosabowski, regarded enemy forces; what were they and most importantly where were they? Sadly this concern was not shared further up the command chain, which seemed to believe the Germans were on the back foot and close to collapse. On the plus side the airborne troops were fit, well trained, well led at lower command levels and highly motivated. Whilst this alone would not win a battle in a modern setting, it would provide the enemy with more than a scrap.

A portent of things to come? One of the gliders used by the British is seen alight after landing near Arnhem. (ADN Picture Archive)

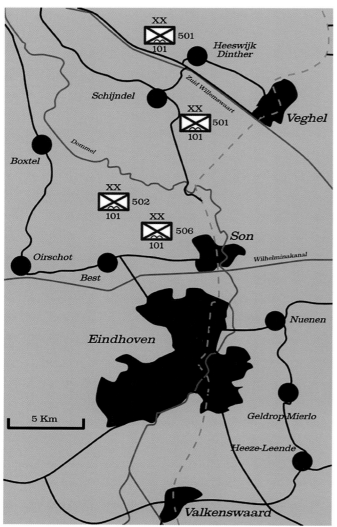

The 101st's landing zones were mercifully close to their objective and the advancing armour of XXX Corps. By nightfall on 18 September the leading elements of XXX Corps would be supporting the paratroopers and throwing a Bailey bridge over the Wilhelminakanaal.

In what had had become a signature move by Montgomery Market Garden was a shock and awe assault on the exhausted Germans. Twenty thousand paratroopers, well trained and ready to fight, were taken to their drop zones by 2,000 aircraft and 500 gliders. Alongside flew fighter escorts and fighter-bombers keen for targets of opportunity.

Soldiers of No. 2 (Dutch) Troop, predecessor to Korps Commandotroepen (the Dutch Commando Corps), prepare for Market Garden. (MoD (Dutch))

The numbers involved dwarfed those of Operation Overlord. Accompanying the paratroopers were over 500 vehicles, 300 artillery pieces and almost 600 tonnes of equipment. The divisions involve knew they might have to fight in isolation for up to four days and were equipped accordingly.

25pdrs of 430 Battery, 55 Field Regiment Royal Artillery, supporting the Guards Armoured Division. (IWM)

On the ground Horrocks and his Garden force waited at Neerpelt, Belgium, with some 23,000 vehicles which included 2,300 engineering vehicles, and 50,000 troops all straining at the leash ready to surge forward. With Eindhoven only 22km (14 miles) away it must have seemed that Montgomery's gamble would work. The tanks of the Guards Armoured Division would lead the advance, their place in the plan being simple: if they encountered an obstacle then the 43rd, the follow-on division, would take over and lead the assault with the Guards maintaining flank integrity. At midday the brakes were off and XXX Corps advanced towards Eindhoven and 101st Division.

The 101st had made landfall perfectly. Their training was paying off and within two hours of landing the 501st Parachute

Parachutes open. Paratroopers during the operations of the 1st Allied Airborne Army in Holland. September 1944. (US Army)

Hammer of the Gods. A Typhoon is rearmed at a forward airfield. (HMSO)

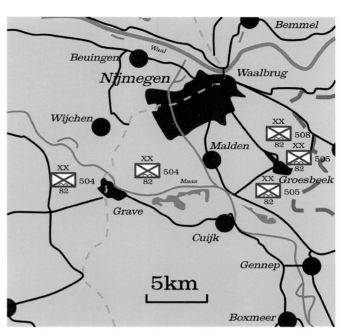

Infantry Regiment (PIR) had secured the Veghel canal bridges. At Drommel the 502nd PIR had secured their bridge and by early afternoon the 101st had succeeded in capturing multiple canal crossings. However, the 101st weren't having it all their own way with 506th PIR meeting determined resistance at

The 82nd's drop zones were spread along a long line in an area defended by highly-motivated German troops. The fighting, often hand-to-hand, would be both hard and brutal for all sides.

A Bren Gun Carrier leads German prisoners after 158 Brigade's night attack on 17/18 September 1944. (IWM)

German prisoners of 82nd (US) Airborne Division from Nijmegen and the surrounding area. (IWM)

Son 9km (5.6 miles) north of Eindhoven. Overcoming this, they advanced towards their objective, the bridge over the Wilhelminakanaal, which was literally within their grasp before it was blown by the German defenders.

At 1415hrs the artillery began their rolling barrage of German defensive positions with 300 guns supported overhead by no less than seven squadrons of RAF Typhoons who stalked the skies above the axis of advance. At 1435hrs tanks of the Irish Guards rolled on and advanced. Initial contact was light machine-gun fire, but then without warning nine tanks were destroyed by a hidden 88mm in the anti-tank role. The road upon which they advanced stood proud to the surrounding marshland, which not only elevated the advancing armour, making them stand out, but also provided cover for enemy troops, something that was discovered by the escaping tank crews. In one instance the surprise was so complete that the two adversaries simply sat and shared a smoke.

Aside from the elevated position of the road it was also narrow, with barely enough room for two vehicles to pass, and cross-country passage over the marshland was out of the question. This would be an issue in itself as damaged vehicles would have to be shunted off the road, and to do that required slow-moving bulldozers. Finally a combination of infantry and air support soon cleared the defenders and the Irish Guards advanced once more towards Eindhoven, but continued contact with enemy forces, including knocking out an SP gun, had seen Horrocks's initial ETA of 1700hrs evaporate. By nightfall the fighting has lessened and the Irish Guards laagered for the night, their peace occasionally disturbed by the odd shot and surrendering Germans who were pointed in the direction of the Brigade HQ.

For Gavin and his 82nd the day had started well, and like the 101st they had made near perfect landfall along with Browning who was commander of the Market forces. On landing, the

505th and 508th PIRs captured the strategically-important town of Groesbeek and part of the heights there. To the south the 504th assaulted and took the bridge over the Maas as well as several canal bridges, while the 2nd Battalion assaulted the bridge at Grave. Here they were met by murderous fire from a 20mm flak gun in the close support role. Eventually the gun was captured and subsequently used against the remaining defenders. By mid-afternoon the bridge was secured. Elsewhere the 508th regrouped and advanced toward the Nijmegen Bridge, but this was well defended by armour and the attack stalled 400m short of the objective.

At 1300hrs the 1st British Airborne Division started to arrive at Arnhem. Even though the drop zone was 10km (6 miles) from the actual town, such was the confidence in their plan that some officers had even brought their No. 2 Service Dress for what they believed would be the inevitable victory parade. To help close the considerable distance between the drop zone and objective, jeeps had been brought along to seize the bridge in a *coup de main*, but sadly half the jeep force and its commander Major Freddie Gough had been seemingly lost to anti-aircraft fire. Another issue was lack of radio communication with the outside world, which was the result of poor procedure and underpowered radio sets. That said, William of Orange, a carrier pigeon, was eventually dispatched with a message explaining the communications situation and the need for assistance. He arrived four hours later, in his loft in Cheshire, after flying some 418km (260 miles).

General Urquhart split his forces, with 1st Parachute Brigade advancing onto Arnhem and 1st Airlanding Brigade remaining at the drop zone to provide security. The Germans were quick to respond and mobilized to engage the landing force, but the paratroopers had split into three groups, and the one headed by Lieutenant Colonel John Frost took a different route to the objective which bypassed the heaviest of the

Four men of 1 PARA, 1st (British) Airborne Division, take cover in a shell hole outside Arnhem, 17 September 1944. (IWM)

German resistance. Once in Arnhem, Frost and his battalion established a foothold at the north end of the bridge with plans to advance to the south end with reinforcements, once they arrived. Miraculously the lost Major Gough and his jeeps appeared along with the anti-tank guns.

Unbeknown to the British, they had landed in an area occupied by the 9th and 10th SS Panzer Divisions who were regrouping. On top of this the Germans had recovered the plans of the entire operation from the body of a dead paratrooper at Nijmegen. Surprise was lost.

The first two gliders to touch down at the British drop zones are unloaded. Note the signaller in the rear of the jeep and the how the two gliders have collided. (IWM)

Waffen-SS prisoners, 18 September 1944. Their presence hadn't been fully appreciated by planners and would seriously hamper Allied operations. (IWM)

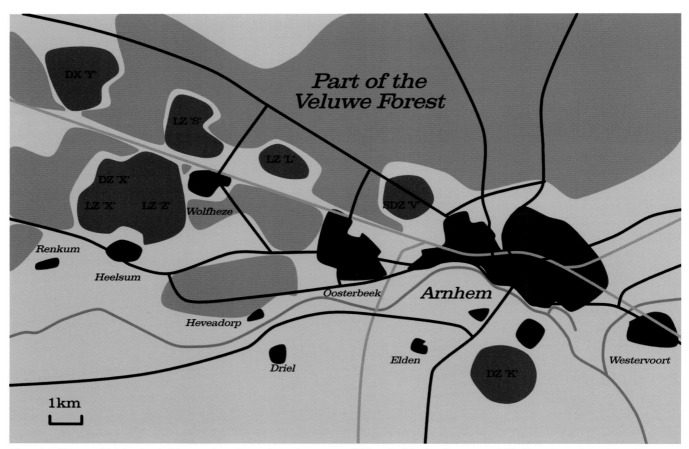

Then 1st Airborne Division landed in a series of parachute drop zones (DZ) and glider landing zones (LZ). The pilots of the Glider Regiment performed virtual miracles in landing in spaces so tight as to be bordering on impossible. The fighting would be brutal as the SS locked horns with the men of the Division.

Staff of the HQ Divisional Artillery of the 101st Airborne Division examine what remains of a glider. (US Army)'.

Republic P-47D Thunderbolts and local guards. These P-47s provided valuable air support for troops on the ground during Market Garden. These aircraft belonged to the 81st Fighter Squadron in the summer of 1944. (IWM)

Once again XXX Corps led by the Irish Guards rolled north towards the 101st at Eindhoven via Valkenswaard, where they continued to meet stiff German opposition. The main force finally made contact with elements of the 101st and Browning that evening on the edge of Eindhoven. During the day the 101st had been reinforced by a further 2,500 personnel mainly from the 327th Glider Infantry Regiment (GIR) in a drop which landed 95 percent of personnel and equipment safely.

This photograph of Royal Engineers constructing a Bailey bridge over the Antwerp-Turnhout Canal in late 1944 shows what a labour-intensive task it was. Now imagine doing this under fire and at night. (IWM)

During XXX Corps' move another bridge over the Wilhelminakanaal, this time at Son, had been damaged to the point that only infantry could cross, leaving commanders with little option but to seek another crossing west across the canal. The 3rd Battalion 502nd PIR were directed to take a bridge near Best but became involved in heavy fighting with a now fully awake defending force made up of troops from the 59th Infantry Division, who fought tooth and nail. Even though they had been reinforced by the 2nd Battalion, the bridge was blown by the defenders. Fighting continued into the afternoon with the Germans bringing up armour which tore into the attacking paratroops. When all seemed lost five P-47 Thunderbolts suddenly appeared, destroying the armour. The battle ended with an impasse and the Americans withdrew to the south-east.

With the arrival of the Irish Guards the 101st had real power, and the Guards were able to move freely along secured roads and soon they had linked up with friendly forces at Son. There the combat engineers worked through the night constructing a Bailey bridge over the Wilhelminakanaal. By morning the work was complete and the armour rolled once more, but it was now more than 30 hours behind schedule. The columns soon reached Veghel. From there they pushed on and met up with the 82nd at Grave before crossing the Maas and the Mass-Waal Canal, where they regrouped south of Nijmegen. Gavin must have been both relieved to finally see the British armour and thankful as a detachment of Coldstream Guards' tanks were attached to the 82nd, ready to engage German armour.

Gavin's troops had not had a great day, fighting heavily against a German counter-attack which had come through the Reichswald, a cross-border area of woodland. The aim

Alongside regular German units were special Kampfgruppe such as this this Radfahrsschwadron (Cycle Squadron), formed from hastily-gathered troops and deployed against the Allied paratroopers. (ADN Picture Archive)

of the attacking forces, over 2,500 men in strength, was to regain control of the Groesbeek Heights. Initially they were successful but a counter-attack by the 508th PIR in the early afternoon, followed by the fortunate arrival of glider-borne reinforcements, shattered the German attack and the 82nd retained the Heights. Meanwhile a company-sized assault force had tried to capture the Nijmegen Bridge, which remained intact, but was beaten back by the defenders of the 10th SS Panzer Division. The following day the Allies returned to the task in hand and moved forwards in three columns, guided by locals, with the intent of capturing the bridge and liberating Nijmegen. Soon the advance began to attract artillery and anti-tank fire which brought it to a standstill.

To the south a reinforced 506th PIR and a squadron of Cromwells advanced eastwards towards Helmond where they encountered a superior German force, including forty tanks from the 107th Panzer Brigade which fielded both Panthers

and StuG IV assault guns. The Germans engaged the 506th, destroying four Cromwells before moving towards a Bailey bridge with the intent of destroying it. This was defended by the 502nd PIR, who fought tooth and nail to keep the bridge intact. Their divisional commander General Maxwell Taylor even got involved, towing anti-tank guns with a jeep to help see off the advancing Germans.

The following day XXX Corps entered Nijmegen. It had taken them three days. The situation at Arnhem was rapidly deteriorating for the British Paras, the 101st were struggling to secure the Helie Highway from frequent German incursions as well as meet their operational objectives and the 82nd were unable to secure the Nijmegen Bridge. The centre was starting to collapse.

A StuG IV assault gun takes a moment to resupply between engagements. (Wydawnictwo Prasowe Kraków-Warszawa)

Sherman tanks of the Irish Guards Group advance past others which were knocked out earlier during Operation Market Garden. (IWM)

In the north, Lieutenant Colonel John Frost and the men of 2nd Parachute Regiment (2 PARA) found themselves isolated on the north side of the bridge at Arnhem. No matter what the Paras did they simply couldn't secure the south side, which was protected by a German pillbox and a far heavier weight of fire than could be realistically countered by Frost and his men.

On the morning of 18 September the German defenders crossed the bridge in force using armour as a spearhead. As they approached the British-held northern bank all hell broke loose with the defenders opening up with their Projectors, Infantry, Anti-Tank (PIATs) and a 6pdr anti-tank gun. The leading vehicles slipped past the anti-tank screen, but ten others were not so lucky. The surviving Germans, from a reconnaissance battalion which had inflicted heavy losses on the 82nd at Nijmegen, sought shelter in a school building which was already in the hands of Major Gough and his men. The ensuing fighting was rough, with Gough in particular enjoying the ensuing melee with him and his men taking retribution for their fallen American brothers in arms from the surprised Germans.

The Germans returned in the afternoon with panzergrenadiers, who engaged the Paras in bitter hand-to-hand fighting, with the Paras making multiple bayonet charges. Thankfully radio contact with the artillery at Oosterbeek has been established and the ensuing fire support helped to drive back the attacking Germans. The fighting had only just begun as 1st Airborne Division began to realize they were up against the 2nd SS Panzer Corps.

Elsewhere 1st Airlanding Brigade, tasked with defending the drop zones, awaited the arrival of 4th Parachute Brigade who were delayed due to poor weather conditions in England, fighting off a Kampfgruppe made up of soldiers, sailors and airmen. The Kampfgruppe had brought six Renault Beute panzers, though these were rapidly destroyed. At the same time 1 and 3 PARA advanced from Oosterbeek with the intent

Men of the HQ Troop of 1st Airlanding Brigade Reconnaissance Squadron at Wolfheze, on the outskirts of Arnhem by the railway line. The man on the left is manning a Projector, Infantry, Anti-Tank (PIAT). (IWM)

Panzergrenadiers working their way along the drainage ditches that ran parallel to the raised road, which provided cover from 1st Airborne Division's positions. (Bundesarchiv)

of breaking through to 2 PARA. However, 3 PARA found themselves pinned down at a road junction by German armour, machine gunners and snipers, whilst SS infantry closed in on their position.

1 PARA fared no better, attracting effective German fire as they approached the outskirts of Arnhem, though a flanking attack helped to drive the Germans back. As it advanced 1 PARA was joined by isolated elements of 3 PARA and together they advanced towards the remainder of 3 PARA at the road

Two airborne soldiers man their wireless trench awaiting contact with the enemy. (IWM)

junction. They were supported by the artillery at Oosterbeek as well as mortar fire from their own battalions. The fighting was brutal with a German counter-attack being repelled at massive cost and still 3 PARA were no closer to reaching 2 PARA, who were perilously close to running out of ammunition. On top of this both the division and brigade commanders, Urquhart and Lathbury, had gone missing, cut off in the confusion of the fighting. Lathbury was then wounded and left in the care of a Dutch couple. He would later escape capture by simply walking out of the hospital he had been confined in. Urquhart and his men sought shelter in the attic of a Dutch family, ready to fight it out, whilst Germans swarmed in the streets below them.

With their commander missing, Brigadier 'Pip' Hicks of 1st Airlanding Brigade, now installed in Model's abandoned HQ of the Hartenstein Hotel, assumed command in what was a very uncertain situation. He knew where 2 PARA were, but had no idea of the exact locations of 1 or 3 PARA. A decision was made to retask 2nd Battalion South Staffordshire Regiment from defending the drop zone to linking up with Frost's 2 PARA. As with 1 PARA's initial advance, the 2nd South Staffords met with stiff resistance as the Germans continued to pour men and material into the area, recapturing lost ground from the lightly armed airborne troops as they did so.

By mid-afternoon 4th Parachute Brigade, led by Brigadier John Hackett, had arrived with over 2,000 troops, which had caused the Germans attacking the drop zone to either flee or surrender. Once the 4th organized itself Hackett sent

Fighting in Built-up Areas is the sort of battle every commander wants to avoid, but now the airborne troops were embroiled in deadly close-quarters combat against a determined foe. (IWM)

the 10 and 156 PARAs to take the high ground to the north of Arnhem at Wolfheze, whilst 11 PARA would join and reinforce the 2nd South Staffords and 1 PARA at Arnhem. They finally linked up with 1 PARA, with commanding officer Lieutenant Colonel David Dobie planning another attempt to reach Frost in the morning. In the meantime Hackett went to the Hartenstein Hotel where a confrontation between him and Hicks ensued over which unit should relieve those at Arnhem. Overhead the RAF and USAAF continued to drop much-needed supplies, though most landed in German-held

Indirect fire support was provided by mortars on both sides. Here British paratroopers respond to a fire mission on enemy positions on the banks of the Rhine. (IWM)

A camouflaged German quadruple anti-aircraft gun on a towing vehicle with a trailer near Arnhem. These simple weapons could create havoc among the slow-flying supply planes. (Bundesarchiv)

Allied planes dropping supplies to German troops. (Bundesarchiv)

territory. This territory was now making the Oosterbeek area a container for the British paratroops, held by seven battalions of panzergrenadiers, military police and naval infantry.

The following morning plans were drawn up with the 1st Parachute Brigade trying once more to reach and support 2 PARA, whilst 4th Parachute Brigade would take and hold

Soldiers of the 2nd Battalion, South Staffordshire Regiment advancing on the Oosterbeek and Arnhem road. (IWM)

the Lichtenbeek feature, high ground to the north-west of Arnhem.

The reinforced 1 and 3 PARA would follow the bank of the Rhine south towards Arnhem, while 11 PARA along with two companies from the 2nd South Staffords would advance along the main road. The 1st and 3rd were soon spotted by members of the 20th SS-Panzergrenadier Regiment and the two forces clashed, often fighting hand-to-hand with bayonets. During the course of the fighting the force ran out of ammunition for their anti-tank weapons, and was soon swamped by German armour. Sadly both PARA battalions also lost their commanding officers. Dobie was captured whilst sheltering from enemy fire and 3 PARA's Lieutenant Colonel John Fitch

SS Panzergrenadiers and Fallschirmjäger outside Arnhem. At this point the noose is tightening around 2 PARA with no relief in sight. (Bundesarchiv)

German soldiers advance under cover towards British positions. (Bundesarchiv)

was killed by a mortar round. 11 PARA and the South Staffords were also caught up in bitter fighting as they advanced into Arnhem, and were literally taken apart by intense German fire. The attack was being torn asunder, leaving the streets littered with dead and wounded. 10 and 156 PARA fared no better, being spotted by German artillery as they advanced and being subjected to effective and murderous fire which forced them to stop and dig in short of their objective.

Amid all the chaos emerged a very concerned Urquhart, after a day and half of being away from his HQ at Hartenstein. On arrival he assessed the situation, and was taken aback by the presence of two SS divisions, a challenging communications picture and the worrisome news that XXX Corps had still not reached Nijmegen. By the afternoon the pressure on 1st Airborne Division was becoming unbearable, with 4th Parachute Brigade looking increasingly in danger of being cut off. Finding a suitable gap in a railway and 10 and 156 PARA still under fire, Urquhart ordered the 4th to withdraw.

At the bridge Frost and the men of 2 PARA continued to soak up the punishment meted out to them by the Germans, their perimeter slowly shrinking to a mere ten buildings. From the south bank withering fire rained down on the beleaguered Paras with armour being used in the direct fire role, obliterating the buildings they were sheltering in from a distance, weary of being ambush by the wily defenders.

Slowly this war of attrition took its toll and one by one the Paras began to run out of ammunition, and the bullet was replaced by the bayonet in the numerous close-quarter battles that broke out. The ferocity was merely amplified by the Paras' almost fanatical fighting spirit. Come early evening 2 PARA had beaten back numerous attacks and Frost remained convinced that the Shermans of XXX Corps would arrive at any moment.

At Oosterbeek railway station the remaining 400 men of 1, 3 and 11 PARA and the survivors of the two companies of the 2nd South Staffords prepared a composite force known as 'Lonsdale Force' led by Major Richard Lonsdale of 11 PARA. The force would defend the eastern side of the Oosterbeek box. Meanwhile the 4th Parachute Brigade had crossed the railway line at Wolfheze and was making their way back to the rest of the division. Urquhart was now faced with a terrible decision, and having no choice he abandoned plans to relieve Frost and concentrated on reinforcing the defences of the box which he and his men found themselves in. Over in England the men of the Polish Parachute Brigade, with their commander Major-General Stanisław Sosabowski, waited impatiently for the order to emplane and reinforce their comrades at Arnhem.

This day would become known as Black Tuesday.

The Nijmegen Bridge was now the focal point for both sides, the Allies needing it to advance and Model refusing to destroy it, insisting on it being held to facilitate a future counter-attack. By the 19th a plan to cross the well-defended bridge was being formulated by Browning, Horrocks and Gavin, and although radio communications with 1st Airborne Division at Oosterbeek were virtually non-existent they prepared themselves for the worst. Their plan, launched the following day, would open the bridge and allow the Guards Armoured Division to race north, link up with Urquhart and his men and take Arnhem Bridge intact.

Members of the Dutch Resistance with troops of the 326th Medical Company, 101st Airborne. (CIA)

The plan was as daring as it was dangerous with men from the 505th PIR advancing through the city supported by armour and infantry from the Grenadier Guards Group. Whilst this was going on, men from Gavin's 82nd would cross the Waal in light canvas and wood assault boats 2km (1.3 miles) west of the road bridge, assaulting the enemy-held bank in a daring river crossing supported by direct fire from the Irish Guards' armour and British and American artillery. Initially planned for the hours of darkness, Gavin had to wait as the boats were

somewhere in the vast tailback that was XXX Corps' stalled advance. On top of this the 82nd had no experience whatsoever in using assault boats. Given time was of the essence the decision was made to essentially unload the craft upon arrival and start the crossing immediately, and the assault on the bridge would begin simultaneously.

On the morning of the 20th, as the 2nd Battalion 505th PIR and Grenadier Guard Group began their advance against defending troops from 10th SS Panzer Division, the Germans struck out from the Reichswald in a coordinated assault. They attacked Groesbeck as well as Mook and Berg-en-Dal and several lightly defended villages in the area. Initially the German assault did well, but the offensive spirit of the 505th PIR and the Coldstream Guards stemmed the assault and by early afternoon they had beaten back the advancing Germans.

A Sherman of the 4th/7th Dragoon Guards passes a knocked-out Panzer III in Oosterhout near Nijmegen. (IWM)

At Nijmegen the pressure of the Allied advance was becoming too much for the Germans who were slowly being pushed back towards the bridge. To the west the US 504th PIR, led by Colonel Rueben Tucker, prepared to cross the Waal led

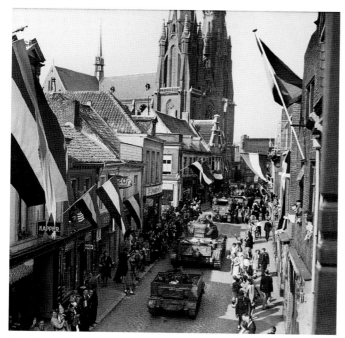

Crowds welcome Cromwell tanks of 2nd Welsh Guards as they enter Eindhoven. (IWM)

British infantry carrying lightweight canvas assault boats ready to cross the Meuse-Escaut canal, 19 September 1944. These boats would be rushed over to Tucker's 504th the following day. (IWM)

by the 3rd Battalion followed by the 1st. As the supporting armour and artillery prepared itself, RAF Typhoons began softening up the northern bank and by 1430hrs the armour and artillery were joining in as well as sustained-fire weapons. A smokescreen, which would prove to be ineffective, was also laid down. Once the boats arrived the men of the 504th, casting all doubts aside, took the freshly-assembled boats and began to cross the 350m-wide river, often using rifle butts to propel the flimsy craft through the water.

Initially the assault was a surprise to the German defenders, and whilst the bank hadn't been subject to the defensive measures that were the usual hallmark of German commanders, it was still a formidable obstacle and well defended by machine guns, mortars and 20mm Flak guns, so the ensuing wall of hot metal that tore into the advancing boats was almost completely effective in stopping that first wave. As a result over half the boats were lost, but the 3rd Battalion landed and soon established a beachhead on the northern bank. Thereafter a further five crossings were made, all observed by Horrocks and Browning, who was heard to remark, 'I have never seen a more gallant action'.

the east. On arrival at the railway bridge two companies of the 3rd ran into stiff opposition, and initially the advance looked as though it would falter, but the appearance of the 505th PIR and the Grenadier Guards attacking from the south threw the defending Germans into a panic. Chaos reigned supreme as the fleeing Germans fell under the murderous fire of the 3rd Battalion. Elsewhere the artillery positions at Fort Hof van Holland were assaulted and taken by men of the 3rd Battalion.

On the south side of the river the combined Guards and paratrooper force began their assault on the road bridge. Initially met by stiff resistance, the capture of the Valkhof, an old fort, by the infantry gave the attackers an edge, and allowed them to fire on the bridge's defenders. Before dark the Allies reached the bridge embankments and to effect a link-up four Shermans of the Grenadier Guards raced forward, led by Sergeant P. Robinson. Suddenly the bark of an 88mm was heard and Robinson's tank was hit. Miraculously the round failed to destroy the tank, which withdrew to the shelter of a bank, but it did destroy his radio. Whilst Robinson exchanged tanks with a fellow Grenadier, Lance Sergeant Pacey, advanced and destroyed the offending 88mm. Suddenly all hell broke loose with the Grenadier Guards being fired upon by all manner of anti-tank weaponry, including Panzerfaust.

A Sherman tank of 13/18th Hussars by the River Waal at Nijmegen gives an idea of how wide the crossing was and how exposed and exceptionally brave the men of the 504th were. (IWM)

This photo of an 88mm emplacement shows not only how easily they were camouflaged but also the gun's crew. Crews like this were well drilled and highly motivated. (Bundesarchiv)

On the northern shore the fighting was now hand to hand, with the Americans swarming the German positions, defended by teenagers and old men, with unparalleled ferocity and violence, eager to avenge their fallen comrades. By 1600hrs the 504th had a 1,000m-deep foothold on the northern bank and were advancing towards both the road and railway bridges to

As they advanced across the bridge 10th SS Panzer Division's commander, General Heinz Harmel took the decision to destroy it and the four Shermans crossing it. Ordering the engineer to blow the bridge, Harmel panicked as nothing happened and repeated strikes of the detonator failed to produce the destruction he so keenly sought. But the advancing Grenadier Guards could not be stopped; even the concrete blocks which were positioned at the northern end of the bridge were nudged aside, with XXX Corps linking up with the paratroops. The arrival of Robinson and his troop was vindication of the plan, with the men of the 504th deservedly taking the laurels for their élan.

The Grenadier Guards, including the future Secretary General of NATO Captain the Lord Carrington, advanced towards the village of Lent where Harmel had watched the crossing by Robinson and his troop. Meanwhile the Irish Guards arrived to secure the bridgehead on the northern bank, thus allowing the advance to Arnhem to continue. Yet the armour stood fast. The American paratroopers were as horrified as they were mystified. They were desperate to advance and link up with their British and Polish brothers in arms.

Tanks of British XXX Corps cross the bridge at Nijmegen during its capture. (IWM)

Thankfully Gavin arrived on the scene before things became complicated and explained to a very exasperated Tucker that

A Sherman Firefly at Bovington Tank Museum, painted to represent Sergeant Robinson's tank, the first to cross the Waal at Nijmegen. (TM)

Meanwhile at Arnhem. A soldier provides supporting fire from an SdKfz 250/1. Note the supply parachute behind him. (Bundesarchiv)

the Guards were committed to ensuring Nijmegen was secure and would be unable to move until the following morning. Thanks to continued German attacks on the Helie Highway, which were disrupting XXX Corps' supply lines, the Guards Armoured Division in particular were beginning to run low on ammunition and fuel. This needed to be addressed, and replacement infantry, who would be the spearhead of any advance on Arnhem, had to arrive before any meaningful advance could take place.

To further complicate matter the geography now played a part in tactical planning; the road from Nijmegen to Arnhem continued to be embanked. It was also flanked by woodland, allowing for effective snap ambushes and well-hidden defensive positions to be organized. Horrocks now planned to throw the 43rd Wessex Division into the fray as the lead infantry division, leapfrogging ahead of the Guards Armoured Division. The 43rd, however, were stuck in the corps-sized traffic jam behind Nijmegen. When 130th Infantry Brigade of the 43rd arrived at Grave that night they had to fight off repeated German attacks, and Horrocks had no choice but to let them rest before they continued. Meanwhile Browning was in communication with Urquhart, promising the relief column would leave for the 1st Airborne Division the following day.

A welcome liberator. An Irish Guardsman accepts a cigar from a Dutch gentleman welcoming his liberation. (Nationaal Archief)

All dressed up. The 43rd Wessex Division would struggle to make headway along the narrow road of the advance and as a result were often delayed by traffic jams. (IWM)

To the north, the relief attempt by Lonsdale Force had failed in the face of ever-increasing German pressure, but Frost and the men of 2 PARA continued to fight and wait for the arrival of XXX Corps. For Urquhart the situation was rapidly deteriorating; his division was simply being lined up for obliteration by superior German forces. Taking stock of the situation around Oosterbeek, he ordered Hackett and 4th Parachute Brigade return as soon as possible. Given the brigade was still fighting, a withdrawal plan was organized with 10 PARA as vanguard with 156 PARA providing rear cover. Urquhart realized his priority was to maintain the Oosterbeek bridgehead and as a result he had to take his hardest decision; to stop any further attempts to relieve 2 PARA.

The situation around Oosterbeek was deteriorating at a rapid pace and soon the gunners of 'D' Troop, 2nd Battery, 1st Airlanding Light Regiment were firing their 75mm howitzers over open sights. (IWM)

Men of 'C' Company 1st Battalion, Border Regiment, waiting to repulse another attack by an enemy who were barely 90m away. (IWM)

In Arnhem 2 PARA found themselves hemmed into a small area, seeking shelter in ruins and cellars, with a grim determination to stop German advances onto and across the bridge. However, their defensive perimeter continued to shrink under German pressure, and finally the only building remaining in 2 PARA's

hands was its HQ in whose cellar sheltered 200 wounded. That afternoon Frost was wounded and the ever-belligerent Major Allison Digby Tatham-Warter assumed command. Tatham-Warter was renowned for carrying an umbrella as a result of not recalling passwords and this served as an easily-recognizable means of identification. He went on to disable the driver of an armoured car with the tip of the umbrella, poking it through the driver's vision slit and catching his eye. He also used bugle calls to communicate among his troops as he had foreseen difficulties with the radios. His fearlessness was his most remarkable trait, eschewing a helmet for his Para's red beret although this was in turn cast aside for a bowler hat which he wore whilst leading a bayonet charge. At the bridge Major Gough assumed command of the few troops there, feeding back all situations developments to Frost.

The Germans, sensing the Paras' lack of anti-tank weaponry, forced three tanks through their lines and onto the bridge, thus laying it open for the passage of reinforcements. This left the defending Paras little choice but to leave their defensive positions at the school building close to the bridge ramp and attempt to return to the main body. Some managed to break through to their comrades, though most were captured.

A German soldier navigates a narrow footbridge near Arnhem. (Bundesarchiv)

The pressure was being also being applied to 1st Airborne Division at the Oosterbeek bridgehead, where, augmented by glider pilots and members of the Dutch Resistance, it was being pummelled by withering artillery fire, combined with infantry and armour attacks. The remains of 156 PARA, some forty men, launched a bayonet charge led by Hackett and broke through the German lines and reached Oosterbeek, much to Urquhart's relief. The newly-arrived remains of 4th Parachute Brigade were sent to reinforce the perimeter. Combined with

1st Airborne Division soldiers use parachutes to signal to supply aircraft from the grounds of the Hartenstein Hotel. (IWM)

The grave of a British soldier alongside the wreckage of his jeep near Arnhem. (IWM)

the news of the Nijmegen assault the men of the 1st should have been elated. However, the issue with communications remained and in a resupply of vital equipment, nearly all of the seventy planeloads were dropped into German-held territory.

By the evening the situation at Arnhem was bleak and a decision to ask for a truce was made regarding the wounded men in the HQ cellars. These were weakened by at least three fires and the continuing German assault. Whilst the wounded were evacuated the Germans shored up their positions, the Paras doing likewise, though the territory which they held was now real estate, and most of that was on fire. Now out of food, water and ammunition, the situation was indeed desperate and the wounded Frost gave Gough permission to break out and make contact with the main force at Oosterbeek.

Once the truce had ended, and Frost had been taken away with the rest of the wounded, the Germans sent in the 21st SS Panzergrenadier Regiment augmented by Tiger tanks. The Paras fought on until the early hours of 21 September, when the Germans finally got the upper hand. Some were able to escape to Oosterbeek, but most were captured and even then tried to fight on. The SS in particular were weary of these soldiers who they now saw as 'exceedingly dangerous'. The final radio transmission from Arnhem would simply say; 'Out of Ammunition. God Save the King!'.

Captured British paratroopers at Arnhem await their fate. (IWM)

At Oosterbeek Urquhart had lost radio contact with 2 PARA, and although not entirely certain as to why, was more concerned with the defence of his own perimeter. After four days his division was now only 3,000 men strong and all it would take would be one final serious assault by the surrounding Germans. Yet it didn't come. Instead the attacks were small and easily repulsed and by 21 September the division was able to call on XXX Corps' artillery, in particular the long-range medium guns. The almost pinpoint accuracy of the fire support provided by the gunners was most welcome. At the same time word was sent that the Guards Armoured Division was on its way, along with Sosabowski's Poles.

This soldier of 5th Duke of Cornwall's Light Infantry, 43rd (Wessex) Division, carries a PIAT, a versatile weapon that could be used in a variety of roles. (IWM)

As well as the Poles, Dutch troops took part in Market Garden. These men of the Prinses Irene Brigade make a careful advance in their Lloyd Carrier. (IWM)

By mid-morning XXX Corps was rolling again, with the Irish Guards taking point and heading for Arnhem. Initially the advance, supported by RAF Typhoons, went well, but the Germans had established an anti-tank screen in the woodland bordering the elevated road. The initial contact saw the Irish lose four tanks and the Forward Air Controller was unable to contact the Typhoons loitering overhead, who had strict instructions to only respond to his fire missions, due to a damaged radio. The column now halted a mere 10km (6 miles) from Arnhem to await the arrival of the infantry of the 43rd Wessex Division, which was still stuck in traffic.

By the afternoon Sosabowski's Poles were on their way to their drop zone at Driel. En-route Sosabowski could clearly see German armour crossing the bridge at Arnhem, and realized 2 PARA had been unsuccessful in its mission to secure the bridge. Upon landing the Poles had been greeted by stiff German resistance, and on regrouping Sosabowski became aware that his 1st Battalion had failed to make the drop, due to bad weather.

With only half his men he faced Kampfgruppe Knaust, made up of elements from 10th SS-Panzer Division supported by twenty-five Tigers and twenty Panthers. To further complicate matters the vital Heveadorp ferry which could be used to cross the Rhine could not be found. A liaison officer resorted to swimming across the Rhine and reporting to Sosabowski that with the ferry gone, rafts would be sent to help transport the Poles across the Rhine later that night. By the early morning of 22 September there was still no sign of the rafts and the Poles were isolated and unable to assist their brothers in arms on the northern side of the Rhine.

A 2cm Flak gun crew watches for an enemy that never came. (Bundesarchiv)

Finally, reconnaissance elements of XXX Corps made contact with the Polish paratroopers at Driel, having travelled via local back roads. This was a positive moment in another deepening crisis of confidence in Montgomery's plan. To the south the 43rd would follow in an advance which would see the its two brigades split. The 129th Infantry Brigade would push on towards Elst and Arnhem, whilst the 214th Infantry Brigade would progress west towards Oosterhout and on Driel.

Advance to contact! Purposeful-looking British infantry hitch a ride on a Sherman. (IWM)

The attack, which started under the cover of morning fog, was slow and lacked the dash required to make a serious impact on any of the German defenders and by early morning it had been effectively stopped. As Elst was resolutely defended by members of the SS supported by armour General Gwilym Thomas, GOC 43rd Division, changed tack and concentrated his efforts to pushing on through Oosterhout.

Inspecting a broken enemy. A soldier crouches near a knocked-out Panzer III in Oosterhout. (IWM)

Parallel lives. Men of 8th Rifle Brigade hand out chocolate to Dutch civilians during the advance of 11th Armoured Division, part of VIII Corps. (IWM)

At the same time the Germans struck north of Eindhoven near Veghel in an action that effectively severed the main axis of the Allied advance. The only defenders were a battalion of the 501st PIR of the 101st. There should have been flank support from VIII and XII Corps, which would have prevented this audacious action by Model, but they were still held up in the Son area, leaving Veghel exposed.

The fighting was vicious as the men of the 501st clashed with units of the 59th Infantry Division with the 107th Panzer Brigade and 280th Assault Gun Brigade who stormed southwards towards the lightly defended Veghel. They tore along a 14km (8.6-mile) corridor between Uden and Veghel, which would see this stretch of road become known as 'Hell's Highway'. Their assault also prevented the transport of vital supplies north, thus slowing the rescue dash to the men of 1st Airborne Division. Model's timing was perfect.

Thankfully members of the Dutch Resistance had been able to inform General Maxwell Taylor of the 101st that the Germans were coming, which gave the 506th time to prepare their defences. To their credit their efforts stopped the German advance 1,000m short of their objective of the Veghel canal bridge. The defenders were soon supported by armour from the Grenadier Guards, and reinforced by the Coldstream Guards arriving on the morning of 23 September.

A Panther awaits its prey. (IWM)

A member of the Partisan Action Netherland (PAN) guides British troops in locating enemy positions. (IWM)

To the north the 214th were making headway, and supported by divisional artillery broke through the German defenders, capturing Oosterhout. A column of infantry and armour was then dispatched to support Sosabowski's Poles at Driel, arriving in the early evening. This in turn allowed the Poles to start crossing the Rhine with supplies and men to help support the 1st Airborne Division at Oosterbeek, which was now constantly under fire by the Germans, who now had orders from Hitler to annihilate the defenders. However, the arrival of elements of the 43rd gave Urquhart an opportunity to send his chief of staff, Lieutenant Colonel Charles Mackenzie, over the Rhine to explain the seriousness of the situation to Browning and how close to collapse the division was. At the meeting Browning could have been left in no doubt as to the severity of the situation the 1st faced at Oosterbeek, yet Mackenzie could not help but feel that Browning did not really comprehend how serious things really were.

Using a captured Allied machine gun, these Fallschirmjäger hold part of the high ground around British positions at Oosterbeek. (Bundesarchiv)

Meanwhile Model's attack on 'Hell's Highway' was creating havoc and misery. The 107th was now joined by Kampfgruppe Walther and the 6th Fallschirmjäger Regiment, who were tearing into the men of the 101st. The offensive had disrupted supplies to the point where the gunners supporting the 1st Airborne Division at Oosterbeek were in real danger of running out of ammunition and the wounded were unable to be evacuated. At Oosterbeek the Germans were now using self-propelled guns to fire indiscriminately into the built-up

areas where civilians remained, huddled for safety in cellars. By nightfall the 43rd Division were able to provide the Poles with the means to cross the Rhine and join their beleaguered brothers in arms. Only a company were able to cross, however, doing so under heavy fire.

Model's riposte. Soldiers of the 9th SS Panzer Division ride a StuG III through the streets of Arnhem as part of the German counter-attack. (IWM)

The following morning Sosabowski joined Browning and Thomas at Horrocks's HQ to discuss the situation at Oosterbeek and it was decided that more troops would be sent over the river to support the 1st. The remaining Poles, much to Sosabowski's dismay, would now be placed under the command of 43rd Division and would cross the river that night with members of the 130th Infantry Brigade. After this meeting Horrocks and Browning had a further conference with Dempsey to discuss the situation the 1st Airborne were in and the only viable option available was to evacuate neatly 5,000 men from the Oosterbeek pocket. Dempsey then approached Montgomery, who upon realizing the desperation of the situation agreed to the evacuation, and in doing so signalled Market Garden had reached its operational limit.

Throughout Sunday the Germans strengthened their positions around Oosterbeek with Tigers from the 506th Heavy Panzer Battalion, whilst in the afternoon a local truce allowed the evacuation of nearly 500 wounded paratroopers to medical facilities.

This Tiger II of the 506th was finally destroyed at Oosterbeck by the combined fire of a 6pdr anti-tank gun, 75mm howitzer and PIAT. (HMSO)

The following morning, almost three hours late, the Poles and men of the 4th Dorsets started to cross the Rhine, often under withering fire from the Germans on the opposite bank. Like the 82nd's crossing the Waal, they used anything to propel the assault boats, which landed a mere 200 men, who were then able to make contact with elements of the 1st. Among this party was a letter containing details of an operation to evacuate the remaining men of the 1st. Urquhart signalled Thomas agreeing to the evacuation of his men that evening.

Surrounded by the detritus of war, a wounded man is carried away from the Divisional Administration Area by stretcher at Oosterbeek, September 1944. (IWM)

The evacuation, codenamed Operation Berlin, took place under the cover of night. Silently the men of the 1st Airborne Division slipped from their positions and withdrew to the northern bank of the Rhine to waiting boats. The withdrawing soldiers carried nothing but their personal weapons, whilst those wounded who were capable of still holding a weapon remained in the firing positions ready to launch feint volleys of small-arms fire to throw the Germans off the scent. The Corps

Glider pilots pose in front of a Horsa glider. From left: Lieutenant J.F. Hubble; Staff Sergeant B.L. Morgan; Staff Sergeant J.L. Crone; Sergeant R. Biagott. Men like this would help guide their fellow airborne soldiers to safety during Operation Berlin. (IWM)

artillery would provide a massive bombardment to cover the withdrawal, whilst the 43rd would carry out a diversionary attack west of Driel. The result confused the Germans into thinking the British were crossing the river en masse. The evacuation started shortly before 2200hrs with 156 PARA and 7th King's Own Scottish Borderers leaving first. Aside for some groups becoming lost and being taken prisoner, the Glider Pilot Regiment guides, helped by heavy rain, managed to get the soldiers to the necessary crossing points.

Often under heavy fire, the evacuation continued throughout the night, with Urquhart and his staff arriving on the south bank shortly after midnight. It continued until early morning, with wounded men smuggled across by comrades desperate not to leave them behind. By the time the operation stopped over 2,000 men, including the Poles, had made it to safety.

Later in the day the advancing Germans were greeted by mostly empty fire positions, small pockets of resistance or wounded men. There was no sign of the main body of the 1st Airborne Division. Urquhart and his men had slipped away. For their valour the men of the 1st Airborne Division would go on to be awarded five Victoria Crosses.

The grave of a British soldier killed at the battle of Arnhem. (IWM)

RAF crew loading food into the bomb bay of an Avro Lancaster as part of Operations Manna and Chowhound, the 'Hongerwinter' famine relief operations. (IWM)

Why we fight. The crew of a Cromwell tank is welcomed by Dutch civilians in Eindhoven, 19 September 1944. (IWM)

Whilst Market Garden had driven a wedge into German-held territory it had failed to deliver the *coup de grâce* Montgomery sincerely believed it would. Antwerp would remain inaccessible to the Allies for a further two months. After evacuation to England the 1st Airborne Division would never recover and would be disbanded at the end of August 1945.

The Dutch civilian population would suffer heavily in the 'Hongerwinter', with food withheld over the hard winter

months as a punishment by the German High Command for perceived collaboration with the Allies during Market Garden. Some 20,000 civilians would starve to death.

Ultimately, in a moment of hubris, commanders failed to recognize that the German defenders, whilst down, were certainly not out and their plans to deliver a killer blow was rushed. German operational experience and the failure to stop the Fifteenth Army from escaping over the Scheldt River in the summer were to prove disastrous for Market Garden.

The Rhine crossed by a Class 40 pontoon bridge in late March 1945. Within six weeks the Allies would be victorious in Europe. (IWM)

37

QUARTERMASTER'S SECTION

The success of every battle depends on a multitude of factors: command and control, logistics and training are prime examples. There is also the question of equipment and its effectiveness in helping the commander on the ground get the job done.

For all sides Market Garden presented challenges. For the Germans a lack of air superiority and equipment meant Allied pilots has complete mastery of the skies, yet on the ground the Panzer V Panther with its lethal 75mm L70 main gun could deal with most armour sent against it. The British fielded the Cruiser Tank Cromwell, fast, agile and also armed with a 75mm main gun, but it lacked the Panther's protection and was vulnerable to the heavier German tanks of the time.

vehicle, capable of carrying up to three passengers as well as a towed load, which could be a gun, trailer or even a Nebelwerfer. Like the Triumph, the Kettenkrad was quick, agile and versatile, especially in an urban environment.

As subjects, the Cromwell, Panther, Triumph 3HW and NSU Kettenkrad are well served by manufacturers, available in a range of scales and media. In the Quartermaster's Stores you'll find a selection of model kits and accessories in key scales. All have their merits, with great potential for conversions as well as super detailing. As new models are always being produced this list is purely contemporaneous and features kits that are available at the time of writing.

Checking you have the right kit is vital. Here two paratroopers adjust their harnesses during a large-scale airborne forces exercise, 22 April 1944. (IWM)

However, due the fast pace of Market Garden and the situation being in constant flux, commanders on the ground needed means of transport that were fast and that were able to exploit their small size. For XXX Corps the Triumph 3HW motorcycle was an excellent tool for carrying messages and orders down the lines of thousands of vehicles that used the Helie Highway. For the Germans, NSU's Kettenkrad was the ultimate liaison

New ways and old school. Although taken in the north-west Caucasus this photo is an excellent example of the Kettenkrad in the field alongside the beasts of burden it was designed to replace. (Archiwa Panstwowe)

INTRODUCTION

As the Guards Armoured Division rolled over their start line on 17 September 1944 they fielded a mix of US and British armour in their ranks as they advanced towards Arnhem. Among them were the Cromwells of the 2nd Battalion Welsh Guards and 3rd/4th County of London Yeomanry (CLY) (Sharpshooters). As the most widely produced of the cruiser tanks, the Meteor-engined Cromwell was also the fastest. However, crews still had misgivings about the Cromwell's ability to take on German tanks such as the Panther, against which its 75mm or 6pdr main gun would do no real damage.

DEVELOPMENT AND DETAIL

Originally produced by Nuffield in response to a Tank Board request in 1940, the Cromwell was the first tank to be fitted with the Merlin-based Meteor V12 engine. The process started with the new engine being tested in Crusader hulls, where its performance had been nothing short of exceptional, giving an estimated speed of 80.5kph (50mph) on testing runs. After consideration of the result of Nuffield's investigations, the Tank Board decided that three tanks would be developed from experiments; the A24, which was a development of the original Nuffield A14 Crusader, the A27L fitted with a Liberty engine and A22 Churchill gearbox, and the Meteor-powered A27M.

Breaking their fast. Men of the 4th CLY, 7th Armoured Division, with their Cromwell, which is awash with details for the modeller. (IWM)

This hessian-camouflaged Cromwell is mobbed by jubilant crowds as it moves through liberated Brussels. (IWM)

Initially the Cromwell had a shaky start to the invasion of Northern Europe, where German Panthers and Tigers, which were able to use the cover of the Normandy Bocage to their advantage, took a heavy toll on the advancing Allied armour. Once the Cromwell was free of the Bocage, however, its role as a cruiser tank came into its own where its speed was its greatest asset. However, it was once more slowed down on the narrow and elevated road to Arnhem, where the Panthers roamed once again, taking their toll on the armour of XXX Corps.

The A27M was clearly the version the Tank Board favoured and the all-important cooling system was perfected over nine months of strenuous testing and design perfection with the result of an improvement in power to the Meteor engine. In spring 1942 the first prototype was delivered for trials, after which orders were placed for the A27M as well as the A27L, in case of Meteor engine shortage, which was a very real concern given Rolls-Royce's focus on aero engine production.

Battlefield repairs on a Cromwell. Note the orientation of the 11th Division charging bull insignia. (IWM)

A Rolls-Royce Mark III Meteor engine at Bovington Tank Museum. (Geni)

A solution was found in a deal brokered between Rolls-Royce and Rover, where Rolls-Royce would take over production of the new W.2 jet engine from Rover, and Rover would take over production of the Meteor. By late 1942 production of the Meteor was under way on the Morris Motors engine lines. Meanwhile there were concerns about the main gun, which needed to be powerful enough to make the Cromwell a worthwhile investment. A 6pdr with only the capability to fire armour-piercing rounds was not acceptable so the development of a 75mm was started in December 1942. This new gun, the 75mm Ordnance Quick Firing (OQF), would be fitted to the Mk IV Cromwell from late 1943.

Captain L. Cotton MM, wearing the Iron Cross, and crew with their Mk IV Cromwell which was fitted with a 95mm Howitzer, 4 CLY. Note the painted pipe-smoking 'Old Bill' character, from another war and a world away, adorning the hull. (IWM)

A full 3,220km (2,000-mile) test exercise was carried out during the high summer of 1943 with the Cromwell pitted against a range of contemporary designs including the US diesel-powered M4A2 Sherman. This highlighted a range of drive train issues, which surprisingly were known about prior

to the test, but additional time was given to the design and manufacturing teams from Leyland to address these. These issues aside, the Cromwell handled well and was liked by its crews.

By early 1944 the production model details had been finalized by Leyland who had made further changes to the design, including welds added to joints to strengthen and seal the hull as well as additional belly armour. In production the Cromwell followed other cruiser tanks in having Christie suspension and was fitted with five road wheels either side. The Cromwell was capable of fording through water up to 1.2m (48in) deep, which would help with unloading from Landing Ships Tank in future amphibious operations.

A Cromwell crew poses with happy children celebrating their arrival at Valkenswaard near Eindhoven, 18 September 1944. (IWM)

By the time of D-Day Cromwell crews were now familiar with their new charges, and those who had swapped their Shermans for the Cromwell found them faster though cramped. Its lower profile helped to conceal the Cromwell, which was welcomed by

When Churchill met Cromwell. (IWM)

Magnanimous in victory; A Cromwell transports German wounded to an aid station. (IWM)

those crews who had come over from Shermans. The ability to fire on the move was also welcome and hydraulically-powered turret traverse motors with proportional speed control were fitted. The 75mm main gun could effectively engage most German armour apart from the heavier tanks. To get around this weakness the Cromwell would often be paired with the Sherman Firefly or A30 Challenger which both mounted the Tiger-killing 17pdr OQF gun.

In total eight marks of the Cromwell were produced with six differently-produced hull types. As well as the standard A27 a combined command/observation post tank was developed featuring a dummy gun and interior space for additional communications equipment.

A new friend. This crewman is happy with his company in this rather damp photograph. Note the water carriers in the background.

A27M (Meteor) Cruiser Tank Mk VIII Cromwell
Specifications:
Type: Cruiser tank
Crew: 5
Weight: 27,941kg
Dimensions:
    Length: 6.35m
    Height: 2.5m
    Width: 2.9m
Armament:
    Main: Mk I–III 6pdr (57mm) gun; Mk IV–VII 75mm OQF gun
    Secondary: 1 x coaxial 7.92mm Besa MG, 1 x 7.92mm Besa MG in front hull
Front hull armour thickness: 76mm (101mm with appliqué plate)
Engine: Rolls-Royce Meteor V12 petrol engine (5F+1R)
Performance:
    Engine: 600bhp
    Speed: 52–64kph
    Maximum range: 278km

CAMOUFLAGE AND MARKINGS

British armour of this period in Northern Europe had settled down to the use of Standard Camouflage Colours (UK) (S.C.C.) 15 Olive Drab. This colour was occasionally overlaid with black stripes (S.C.C. 14 black), and additional camouflage was gained through the use of hessian strips which hung around the turret top. Outclassed by the Panther, Tiger and King Tiger, the Cromwell could rely on its speed, reliability and low profile for some chance of survival. Its 75mm gun could also deal with both the Panzer III and IV series should they cross its path.

Troop Commander, 4 Troop, 'A' Squadron, 15th/19th The King's Royal Hussars, Eindhoven, Netherlands, 19 September 1944. This vehicle has only been on the road for 48 hours, its crew relaxed and refreshed with Bols and beer from the local populace. Thus far their advance, though delayed, has been straightforward and the 35 miles ahead to Nijmegen look clear. The following day the King's Royal Hussars would cross swords with the Panther-equipped Panzer-Brigade 107, losing two of their number to these formidable tanks.

9 Troop, 'B' Squadron, 2nd Battalion (Armoured Reconnaissance) Welsh Guards, Nijmegen Waal Bridge, Netherlands, 21 September 1944. This crew have utilized hessian strips to aid breaking the outline of the hull and turret thus making estimating range that little bit harder. The bridge has now been taken and the Welsh Guards await their turn to cross and push on to the ultimate goal with men from the 82nd Airborne; to relieve the beleaguered Frost and his men at Arnhem. Sadly by now it was too late.

QUARTERMASTER'S STORES

The Cromwell, like a great deal of wartime British armour, has often been the poor relation to its American cousins and largely ignored by the mainstream manufacturers. There are two 1/35 offerings currently available to the modeller, Tamiya's 1997 kit Nr. 35221 and Airfix's 2021 kits Nr. A1373 (Mk IV) and Nr. A1374 (Mk VI), which also feature a small fret of photo-etch.

The Tamiya kits, whilst old, are still wonderful models and present the builder with a straightforward job. Whilst Airfix's offerings give the modeller a more contemporary take, they have notable detailing discrepancies of the road wheels. That said, Airfix have included plastic tracks as well as the traditional vinyl type. Instructions are clear for both and the decals, like the instructions, are well made, clear and help bring the kits alive. With various finishing options both kits can be used to depict a Cromwell anytime from D-Day onwards, including Market Garden.

Even Airfix's 1/76 kit box art is steeped in an action scene reminiscent of Roy Cross's wonderful artwork from the mid-twentieth century.

Tamiya's 1/35 Cromwell maybe 25 years old but can still hold its own in the detail stakes.

For the smaller scale modeller Tamiya have added the Cromwell to their 1/48 model range (Nr. 32528) and Italeri in their 1/56 Warlord series (Nr. 15754). In 1/72 scale the Plastic Soldier Company (Nr. WW2V20027) provide no less than three models in their kit. Airfix also offer a nicely-moulded 1/76 kit of the Cromwell (Nr. A02338) which includes plastic tracks and options for two different versions.

Conversion set masters Accurate Armour have produce a range of mixed media sets in both 1/35 and 1/48 scales for the Cromwell including this magnificent engine bay detailing set (A059).

For those wishing to detail their Cromwells then Accurate Armour have a range of multimedia specials available based on Tamiya's 1/35 and 1/48 kits including a Meteor engine (Nr. A059), D-Day special (Nr. A048k) and updated commander's

Star Decals have produced a wonderful set of Guards Armoured Division decals for those wanting to re-create the perfect Market Garden Cromwell.

cupolas for Tamiya's 1/48 kits (Nr. A48009). Photo-etch masters Aber have produced a range of upgrades for the Tamiya 1/35 kit including a 6pdr barrel (Nr. 35L01) and detailing frets (Nr. 35060); these sets are also available in 1/48 scale.

White metal tracks are available from Friulmodel (Nr. ATL-43) and Masterclub (Nr. MTL35082) whilst resin details are available from Black Dog in 1/35, 1/48 and 1/72 scale and include hessian tape camo (Nr. T72049). There are also a good range of decal sets including 1st Polish Armoured Division 1944–1946 by Arno (Nr. 35410), Royal Marines Cromwell and Centaur Support tanks (Nr. EP2716) by Peddinghaus-Decals and Cromwell and Centaur in WW2 (Nr. 72027) by Bison are all great sets with which you can expand your Cromwell fleet. Faithfully reproduced and nicely printed, these really will bring your models alive.

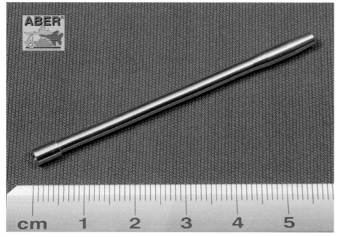

Aber's turned metal 6pdr gun barrel is beautifully made and adds weight to the finely made Tamiya turret.

An excellent front study of Bovington Tank Museum's Cromwell. (Jonathan Cardy)

SHOWCASE BUILD

Tamiya 1/35 Cromwell Mk IV (Nr. 35221), 2nd Battalion Welsh Guards Armoured Recce Regiment, Guards Armoured Division, Nijmegen, 21 September. Build by Geoff Coughlin

The Tamiya Cromwell Mk IV tank is a great kit for anyone who wants a quick and simple build. Fit of parts is excellent as you would expect from this manufacturer. The package includes a figure if you want to add one.

Tracks are the rubber-vinyl one-piece length type and although they fit they are a bit tight and you'll need to adjust the upper run sag for a more realistic appearance. Tow ropes are included and these are made from fabric that's tricky to work with as it frays easily.

There's no doubt that this Tamiya kit looks the part when finished and the machine guns are especially delicate and well formed. The main gun barrel is split and although these can be a pain to clean up, I had no difficulties this time.

Decals included in the kit are fine, if a bit thick and as I was looking something different: markings for 45 Armoured Reconnaissance Regiment, 1944 and Star Decals have the sheet (35-972). My model is built straight from the box.

INTRODUCTION

The Panzer V Panther (SdKfz 171) had its genesis in the early stages of Operation Barbarossa when the German military launched a campaign into Soviet-held territory in Central and Eastern Europe that they truly believed would be over in 12 weeks. Just over 1,000 tanks, mainly 50mm-armed Panzer IIIs supported by the heavier Panzer IVs, crossed over the border with the three Army Groups to face nearly 24,000 significantly weaker Soviet tanks.

A factory-fresh Panther ausf D rolls out from a railhead ready for action. (Bundesarchiv)

If ever there was a display of misplaced confidence then this was it. By late summer the new T-34 medium and KV-1 heavy tanks had been encountered on the battlefield, mercifully for the German tank crews in ones and twos supporting infantry attacks. Even then the shock was total. The German military had little to combat these new battlefield monsters, which could outgun both the Panzer III and IV.

A crew struggle with the removal of one of the many road wheels fitted to the Panther. Note the damaged wheel nearest the hull side. (Bundesarchiv)

A solution was sought which ultimately gave birth to the Panther. It would see service on both the Eastern and Western Fronts, the Panther, freeing up the ageing but proven Panzer III chassis for Sturmgeschütz (assault gun) production. By 1944 the Panzerwaffe may have been on the back foot, but to underestimate them remained a deadly mistake, as the Allies were soon to learn.

DEVELOPMENT AND DETAIL

The Panther was driven by a necessity to counter the hitherto unseen T-34 medium and KV-1s. Members of the German

The 75mm KwK 42 L/70 gave the Panther its bite and could easily deal with any Allied tank that crossed its path on the battlefield. (Bundesarchiv)

tank industry were given a through briefing as well as being allowed to inspect captured examples of T-34s. This briefing took place shortly after the battle of Mtsensk where Soviet armour had engaged their German counterparts for the first time en masse. The resulting battle had been a scare for the Panzerwaffe and a solution was eagerly sought. Time was of the essence.

In fighting trim. This Panther is awash with details for the modeller: note the washing bowl on the turret side. (Bundesarchiv)

The Germans acknowledged that the T-34 in particular was a superior weapon, and its capability to destroy German tanks from ranges of up to 1,000m was as worrisome as its ability to withstand heavy punishment. The father of the Panzerwaffe, Heinz Guderian, gave the closing remarks to the visiting industrialists, laying down the foundations for what he believed would be a suitable countermeasure, a vehicle which was well armed, well powered and well armoured.

Advancing to contact. A Panther passes a stopped companion draped in foliage as camouflage. (Bundesarchiv)

Two companies stepped up to the challenge: Daimler-Benz (DB) and Maschinenfabrik Augsburg Nürnberg (MAN). The objective was to use as much existing technology as possible to keep development time to a minimum. The details were firmed up into a working document, VK30.02, which laid out the weight for the new vehicle, 32.5 tons, along with essential dimensions and armour requirements. By the beginning of 1942 both companies began planning their designs, DB's offering looking exceptionally T-34-like as a result, whilst MAN's was still at the paper stage.

An ausf A of 1st SS Panzer Division 'Leibstandarte Adolf Hitler' passes through a town in Northern Europe. The side armour skirts were often more trouble than they were worth, fouling on scrub. (Bundesarchiv)

On Hitler's orders a commission was established in May 1942 to consider the merits of both designs. After several meetings the commission, headed by Dr Ferdinand Porsche, settled on MAN design which would utilize advances made in a previous

Allied soldiers inspect a destroyed Panther ausf A somewhere in Italy. (Narodowe Archiwum Cyfrowe)

project, including hull design, thus giving the new tank a head start. The new vehicle, which featured torsion type suspension, was considered to be a suitable chassis for the 75mm KwK 42 L/70 main gun mounted in a turret that had been developed as part of the Tiger project, thus saving valuable time. The addition of wide tracks also meant that the Panther would be able to cross softer ground that had been inaccessible to the Panzer IIIs and IVs due to their far narrower tracks. All of this would be wrapped up in a package that whilst mostly off the shelf, would be a well-engineered item whose quality would beat Soviet quantity.

That said, continuous problems with the transmission and steering arrangements would dog the Panther's service life. Towards the end of the war the problems, especially around motive power elements, would mount as quality control suffered as a result of dwindling resources and increased pressure on manufacturing from Allied air raids. At the beginning of 1943 four factories were involved in the production of the Panther with the aim of having 250 ready for the planned summer offensives in the east.

The Valkyries ride on! A Panther pushes on towards the action. (Narodowe Archiwum Cyfrowe)

The first version, the ausf D, was most definitely the product of its rushed birth and experienced the most problems with its fuelling systems and drive train, not helped by the Panther's weight increasing to 43 tons. Initially these Panthers were powered by the Maybach HL210P30 engine which was soon replaced by the HL230P30. Externally the ausf D was fitted with two headlights, later changed to one and turret-mounted smoke dischargers.

Panther ausf A out on the show circuit showing some fine details on the rear hull plate. (Alan Wilson)

This fine colour study of the Panther ausf A not only shows off the tri-colour paint scheme utilized by the German Army from 1944 onward but also the Zimmerit anti-magnetic mine coating. (Besopha)

By August 1943 the ausf D was replaced by the ausf A which featured a range of design refinements including a ball mount replacing the hull-mounted MG's rain flap and a cast cupola for the commander which could mount an air-defence MG 34. Other features included a monocular main gun sight and from September 1943, a coating of Zimmerit anti-magnetic mine paste.

The final version was the ausf G, produced from March 1944 until the collapse of heavy manufacturing in April 1945. This

GIs and war correspondents gather around a Panther ausf D that has come to a sticky end courtesy of P47s belonging to the 366th FG. (Unknown)

This close-up shot shows the construction of the front hull joins as well as the late-war colour scheme. (Dave Highbury)

featured a redesigned hull which offered an increase in armour thickness of 10mm: as a result of this change the driver lost his glacis visor, but was treated to a traversable periscope. Other features included an increase in ammunition load from seventy-eight rounds to eighty-two. Later models were given all-steel wheels and permanently-fitted Schürzen, anti-tank projectile spacer plates that protected the tracks, along the length of the hull.

Other versions included the Bergepanther recovery vehicle and the 88mm PaK 43/3-armed Jagdpanther.

Panzer V Panther (SdKfz 171) ausf G Specifications:
Type: Medium tank
Crew: 5
Weight: 45,500kg
Dimensions:
   Length: 8.9m
   Height: 3.0m
   Width: 3.3m
Armament:
   Main: 75mm KwK 43 L/70
   Secondary: 1 x coaxial 7.92mm MG 34, 1 x 7.92mm MG 34 in front hull and 1 x Nahverteidigungswaffe multi-purpose grenade launcher
Front hull armour thickness: 80mm
Engine: Maybach HL230P30 V-12 TRM gasoline (7F+1R)
Performance:
   Engine: 700bhp
   Speed: 46kph
   Maximum range: 200km

CAMOUFLAGE AND MARKINGS

Panther ausf G, SS-Panzer-Regiment 10, 10th SS Panzer Division 'Frundsberg', Nijmegen, Netherlands, 20 September 1944. 10th SS Panzer Division was quick to react to the arrival of Gavin and the men of the 82nd Airborne, deploying troops to meet the 82nd head on and delay the capture of the key Nijmegen road bridge for 72 hours. Whilst fearsome, these Panthers would have been on an equal footing with the Grenadier Guards' Sherman Fireflies, whose 17pdrs would slice through the Panthers' armour with terrifying ease.

Panther ausf G, Battalion Knaust, 9th SS Panzer Division 'Hohenstaufen', Arnhem, Netherlands, 21 September 1944. This Panther was one of eight that crossed the Arnhem Bridge, along with several StuG assault guns on the morning of 21 September, charged with pushing through the town and on towards the neighbouring town of Elst. As well as carrying the now-universal foliage, which seemed to be applied to any Germany vehicle brave enough to move in daylight, note that this vehicle has retained its Zimmerit anti-magnetic mine coating.

By September 1944 the Panther was a familiar sight on the battlefields of Northern Europe, and had suffered accordingly. Allied air supremacy rendered nearly all daytime movement impossible, leaving commanders and their vehicles sheltering in woodland or barns and moving when only absolutely necessary or at night. On the battlefield, though, the Panther remained a deadly opponent and even though deployed in small numbers, its effect on the morale of those facing it remained marked. Both Panthers are finished in the standard Dunkelgelb (dark yellow) with oversprays of Olivgrün (olive green) and Rotbraun (red brown).

QUARTERMASTER'S STORES

As one would expect, the Panther is exceptionally well provided for when it comes to model kits and accessories. To list every available item would fill a book in its own right so I feel it fair to highlight a selection of kits that would appeal to a range of modellers.

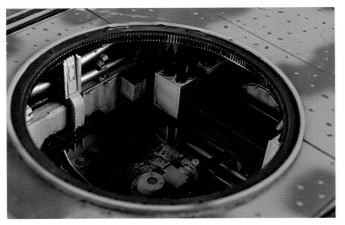

Trumpeter's 1/16 Panther ausf G early version (Nr. 00928) is filled with detailing that will satisfy the most eager and demanding modellers.

For those with the space to spare Trumpter's huge 1/16 2,300 part kit of a late ausf G is a stunning model (Nr. 00928) complete with full interior, finely produced decals and clear instructions. The kit is multimedia and features styrene, photo-etch and milled metal parts, which add to a detail-packed kit, which when complete is roughly four times the size of a 1/35-scale version. The kit is straightforward to build and provides a good challenge to both the returning or new modeller as well as the seasoned hobbyist.

Over the past decade Takom has delivered a raft of armour kits that have wooed modellers and their early Panther ausf G (Nr. 2134), complete with track former and dramatic box art, is no exception.

In 1/35 the range of available Panthers is simply enormous, from Tamiya's ausf D (Nr. 35345) to Airfix's rebox of Academy's late ausf G (Nr1352). These sit alongside Meng Model's ausf A (Nr. 911675) and Takom's full-interior late ausf G (TAK2121) – there is something for everyone. For the smaller scale modeller Tamiya have produced a 1/48 die-cast body ausf G (Nr. 32520) whilst Italeri have added the ausf A to their 1/56 Warlord series (Nr. 15752). 1/72 offerings are also abundant with Dragon making a welcome return with their Panther series including an ausf A (Nr. 7546) which is joined by Revell's ausf G (Nr. 03171). For those really wanting to test their skills, growing Russian manufacturer Zvezda offer the ausf G in 1/100 (Nr. 6169).

There is a huge array of detailing parts in all media available for those wanting to add more detail to their kits in all scales,

Photo-etch masters Eduard have produced a colour detailing PE fret (Nr. 36390) with details for Takom's Panther ausf A (Nr. 2097).

3D-printing concern FC Model Trend have produced a delicate set of exterior tool racks for the Panther.

Star Decals' set for SS Panthers (Nr. 35-C1021) retains the crispness of print and sharpness of colour coupled with well-researched details that has become Star Decals' hallmark.

including Aber's unique 1/16 range and resin masters CMK with their Maybach HL230 P30 engine (Nr. 3110). For those wanting photo-etch, Eduard have numerous sets for all key manufacturers including Academy's ausf G (Nr. 36413). FC Model Trend have produced a series of 3D-printed elements including grill covers (Nr. 35715) and exhausts (Nr. 35589).

Fruilmodel have made a set of their wonderful white metal tracks (ATL-33) whilst Griffon Model have produced a series of photo-etch and turned metal parts (L35001BP). As with all other areas, modellers are spoilt for choice for decals, which can be easily changed to represent Panthers present during Market Garden and are available in a range of scales. Of note are Archer's well researched stencil sets (AR35351), and Star Decals have produced a set for SS Panthers (Nr. 35-C1021).

SHOWCASE BUILD
Tamiya 1/35 Panther Type G, Panzer-Brigade 107, Veghal, Netherlands. Returning modeller Jon Solomon

It has been well over 30 years since I last put together a model kit so building the Tamiya Panther has been a real joy, taking me around five hours over a four-day period. To be honest, it was a bit daunting initially: lots of very small pieces and instructions in numerous different languages made the instructions look detailed and complicated. A few deep breaths later, I got my eye in and the instructions started to make sense. I couldn't wait to get going. Alongside the instructions there was also a 'Tech tips' sheet on preparing and building the model along with painting hints.

After the initial flash of being overwhelmed on opening the box I found that the kit's instructions were simple to navigate, with all the parts fitting together well. Following the instructions meant that I glued the hatches on the turret in a closed position. This negated the option of putting the standing figure into the tank, so he now stands happily on the turret, so all is well. But if I hadn't followed the instructions to the letter, I could have given myself more possibilities.

Before painting I like to sketch designs onto the model. This adds time to the process but will help keep the design in focus as you start to apply your paint. I spent around the same amount of time painting as building (a further five hours). My preference is to 'dry brush' a lighter shade over a painted area to pick out lumps, bumps and detail, giving a 3D effect. This feels like a nice balance between the two halves of the model-making experience. I need to decide which model I will be attempting next.

INTRODUCTION

The Kettenkraftrad (Tracked Motorcycle) was certainly one of the most unique items of equipment used by the Wehrmacht during the Second World War. Initially designed as a light tractor, the Kettenkrad had a presence all of its own, and was capable of crossing a range of obstacles, including the all-important ability to wade through the almost bottomless Russian mud.

An interesting shot of a Kettenkrad with its bespoke trailer somewhere on the Eastern Front. (Bundesarchiv)

Its uses were myriad and by the time of Market Garden it was supporting SS troops who were slowly tightening the noose around 2 PARA at Arnhem and 1st Airborne Division at Oosterbeek. Capable of carrying a variety of loads as well towing a specially-designed trailer or light guns, including 20mm Flak pieces, the Kettenkrad was also employed by the Luftwaffe to tow the Me 262. Captured examples were quickly pressed into service, occasionally receiving a quick coat of Olive Drab paint and a white star for identification purposes.

A Kettenkrad, without its front wheel disks, being inspected by its new owner. (IWM)

After the war the Kettenkrad remained in production with NSU Motorenwerke AG (NSU) for three years and was sold to the farming community as a light tractor fulfilling a range of needs.

DEVELOPMENT AND DETAIL

NSU were approached in 1940 to design and build a new form of halftrack light tractor not exceeding a chassis weight of 500kg that could be carried by the Ju 52 transport aircraft and used to support air assault operations. Given that NSU were producing

a light motorcycle at the time, the 251 OSL, they were able to utilize the technology for the unique steering mechanism which was designed to guide the Kettenkrad around minor obstacles: should the handlebars be pushed beyond 50mm of centre then steering brakes would be applied to the tracks. It was also the single front wheel which gave the Kettenkraftrad its name, though it was physically as far removed from the purpose of a motorcycle as possible. That said, the Kettenkrad often fulfilled roles that would normally be undertaken by a motorcycle and sidecar, from transporting senior officers to the carriage of key equipment. A 35kg capacity trailer, Sonderanhänger 1 (Sd. Anh.1), was also designed to accompany the Kettenkrad.

This Kettenkrad is well stocked with supplies for the front. Note the two rifles hanging from the rear port side and what appear to be artillery rounds in the trailer. (Bundesarchiv)

The Kettenkrad itself carried one driver and two rear-facing passengers. The driver sat on a traditional motorcycle-style seat, with the Opel engine behind him. The clutch and brake pedals were controlled by foot with the gear shift lever sited between his legs. Acceleration was controlled by the traditional motorcycle twist grip on the right-hand side of the handlebars and instrumentation was mounted on a panel set into the main body of the Kettenkrad below the handlebars.

A wonderful view of the controls of a Kettenkrad at the Technik Museum, Speyer, Germany. (Zandcee)

Development was straightforward, although the original motorcycle forks were soon found to be too fragile, with them often broken by crossing rough terrain. This led to the development of a reinforced version, which was also prone to damage. The initial deliveries took place in 1940 and were intended as test subjects for units to develop the platform's use in the field.

The Kettenkrad was a truly remarkable vehicle, capable of working in the most diverse and extreme environments, as show here in the Russian winter. (Bundesarchiv)

Once these tests were completed the Kettenkrad benefitted from several changes including an improved front wheel and fork set, passenger mudguards and a relocated tow hitch. The fork issues wouldn't be resolved until 1942, when a new unit complete with hydraulic shock absorbers was issued.

An excellent view of the forks, front underbelly and tracks. (Yuri Pasholok)

The four-cylinder Opel engine behind the driver must have been a boon in winter. (Yuri Pasholok)

A further weakness was the steering mechanism sealing, which led to the steering brakes becoming fouled with leaking oil, a situation which was alleviated by drains in the steering brake housing. On top of this was the reversing gearwheel, which was easily broken and the resultant debris would affect other parts within the transmission housing.

The Kettenkrad was capable of a good road speed (70kph), could wade up to 440mm and climb a 45° gradient. In fact it possessed remarkable cross-country characteristics, its engine and transmission capable of handling most situations with surprising ease. Pre-production vehicles are easily recognized by their eight-spoked road wheels compared with later six-spoked wheels.

A front three-quarter study view of the Kettenkrad revealing the mass of markings that could be found. (Yuri Pasholok)

Two special line-laying versions were also produced, the SdKfz 2/1 and the 2/2 which laid the heavier cables. On the lighter version the line cable was placed in front of the rear-facing linesman in small reels. The larger carrier would feature reels fitted on to a special jig that sat over the top of the engine, directly behind the driver.

A rear three-quarter study view of the Kettenkrad. Note the exhaust underneath the rear passenger footplate. (Yuri Pasholok)

An interesting close-up of the rear convoy lights. The plate underneath can be raised to display the standard red rear lights. (Yuri Pasholok)

Kettenkrad, SS-Kampfgruppe Krafft, 9th SS Panzer Division 'Hohenstaufen', Oosterbeek, Netherlands, 19 September 1944. Again finished as per the 159th Divisional Supply Group Kettenkrad, this vehicle belongs to SS-Kampfgruppe Krafft, who were among the first troops to engage the British airborne forces in the Oosterbeek area. SS-Kampfgruppe Krafft was made up of replacement SS-Panzergrenadiers who acquitted themselves well initially, but soon the weight of the ever-increasing numbers of British troops forced them back.

Kettenkrads were seen in a variety of finishes and by this stage of the war were often used for tasks that would have been carried out by the SdKfz 250 motorcycle and sidecar combinations. Ideal for liaison, stores and transporting wheeled weaponry, the Kettenkrad's versatility combined with its size and ease of handling cross-country was its advantage.

QUARTERMASTER'S STORES

The Kettenkrad has been a modellers' favourite since Tamiya's first 1/35 offering (MM129) in 1973. This kit was only recently replaced by a new tooled kit (Nr. 35377), again featuring the Kettenkrad and two Landser. As always with Tamiya, both kits

SdKfz2 Kettenkrad Specifications:

Type: Light half-tracked gun tractor
Crew: 1 + 2 passengers
Weight: 1,560kg
Dimensions:
    Length: 3.0m
    Height: 1.2m
    Width: 1.0m
Engine: Opel water-cooled four-cylinder inline engine (3F/1R in 2 ranges)
Performance:
    Engine: 36hp
    Speed: 70kph
    Maximum range: 250km

CAMOUFLAGE AND MARKINGS

Kettenkrad, 159th Divisional Supply Group, 59th Infantry Division, Son, Netherlands, 19 September, 1944. This Kettenkrad has been finished in the standard Dunkelgelb (dark yellow) with oversprays of Olivgrün (olive green) and Rotbraun (red brown). Note the foliage added for increased camouflage whilst laid up. The area around Eindhoven features plenty of woodland, so even the addition of branches to the side of the Kettenkrad broke up the vehicle's shape nicely.

Dragon's 1/6 scale Kettenkrad (Nr. 75001) is awash with the detail and build complexity one would expect from a kit of this size.

are nicely produced and easy to make, though the new tool issue is a welcome change and features sharper detailing.

Tamiya's 1/35 offering was soon followed in 1975 by Esci's impressive 1/9 kit, which features a host of detailing, including opening storage hatches, and is still available in Italeri packaging (Nr. 7404). The kit is one for the seasoned modeller, and features plastic tracks, fine cabling and a detailed Opel engine as well as a well-appointed driver's position along with vinyl seating.

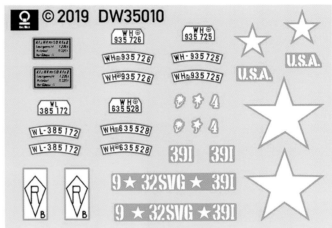

Das Werk's (DW35020) rebox of Dragon's 1/35 Kettenkrad has retained all the former's details and some of its instruction foibles. The option to finish the Kettenkrad as a captured vehicle is a diorama builder's dream too.

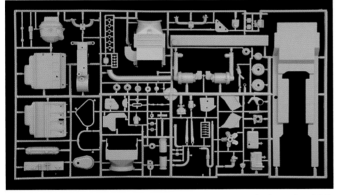

Italeri have constantly flown the 1/9 scale motorcycle-based vehicle flag and the Kettenkrad kit (Nr. 7404), whilst old, is still a worthwhile consideration for the modeller with some experience in motorcycle modelling.

numberplates (Nr. 28503). Spanish concern Minor Models have also produced a range of accessories for 1/35 kits including 3D-printed tracks (VMD35032) and crane set (VMD35073).

Other versions include a multimedia 1/24 scale kit by Fox Model (Nr. K024001) which also comes with the trailer designed specifically for the Kettenkrad and is a wonderful-looking kit aimed squarely at the master modeller. Returning to 1/35, there were numerous Dragon kits produced featuring varying details including a towed Pak 36 (Nr. 6446). This kit is now subject to a rebox by newcomers Das Werk (Nr. 35020) as part of their growing range of kits.

For the 1/48 modeller Tamiya have stepped up once again, providing the smaller scale modeller with an easy-to-assemble model kit. Nr. 32502 features an infantry trailer and Goliath demolition vehicle and trailer. For those wanting to add a 1/72 scale vision to their motor pool Chinese newcomers S-Model (Nr. PS720080) have obliged with a simple, yet rather nicely detailed model kit featuring photo-etch details, including mudguards. Sympathetic dry brushing will help the details of this kit stand out.

For detailing Eduard have produced two photo-etch sets, one for Dragon's 1/35 cable layer (Nr. 3570) and one Tamiya's 1/48 offerings, including a colour fret featuring dials and

Tamiya's new-tool Kettenkrad (Nr. 377) is clearly sharper in appearance to the previous kit, and will make a welcome addition to any modeller's collection.

SHOWCASE BUILD
Das Werk 1/35 Kettenkrad, Unknown unit, Oosterbeek, Netherlands. Ben Skipper

The re-boxing of Dragon's Kettenkrad kit is a bit of a master stroke by Das Werk as it gives modellers access to kits which may not necessarily be available, and given Dragon's somewhat distinctive supply style, it is most welcome. The kit itself is completely unchanged with the sprues retaining the Dragon logo, but the one omission is the beige Dragon tracks which appeared in some kits. This meant building the tracks piece by piece, which wasn't as awkward as I had anticipated, however.

The instructions were visually cleaner than the often chaotic Dragon graphics and processes, that said there are a few errors in numbering parts and I had to cross-refer a couple of times to ensure I had it right. The other little niggle, and Dragon and Das Werk aren't alone in doing this, is not letting the modeller know how many track links are required for each side, forty-three in this case.

Even after 20 years the kit's details remain sharp and the build process straightforward enough. I split the build into two parts: the main body and tracks, and the forks. The fit is more than reasonable, but some filler will be needed a couple of places, I chose to replace the front tow hooks with photo-etch elements as the kit ones seemed a little too large. The fork set is remarkably fiddly, and a magnifying glass was most welcome.

I primed the kit with red automotive primer followed by a coat of hairspray and thinned Vallejo German Cam Beige (70.821). Once dried I used Vallejo Intermediate Green (70.891) for camouflage spray lines and carefully removed sections of the paintwork to reveal scratches and scorch marks. The whole model was sealed with a coat of gloss varnish before adding decals and then a final coat of matt varnish to seal the decals.

INTRODUCTION

The motorcycle is one of the few vehicles that has changed very little over the years. Even now the basics of the motorcycle remain simple and easy to maintain, which have helped make it an essential piece of military equipment.

An Indian dispatch rider competing in an efficiency competition in Cyprus in 1942, on a 3HW. (IWM)

All the bells and whistles. A great example of a re-enactors 3HW at the 2007 Wings over Wine Country Air Show. Final finish details would often change depending on unit, location and usage. (BrokenSphere)

Ridden not hidden. A well-used later 3HW model on display. Note the non-standard chrome plated silencer and the clear headlight lens. (Unknown)

During the Second World War British and Empire forces utilized a range of motorcycles for a variety of purposes, from light reconnaissance, dispatch and liaison tasks to traffic control. Their light weight gave them surprisingly good cross-country performance, and dispatch-riding courses were filled with riders who would often suddenly get closer to nature than they intended as they mastered their skills.

It was in the field that the motorcycles and riders would distinguish themselves and the riders of XXX Corps on the road to Arnhem were no different. One machine in particular that was a firm favourite among them was Triumph's 3HW.

DEVELOPMENT AND DETAIL

The 3HW had its genesis in the work of Triumph's chief designer Val Page, whose previous successes included the stunning Ariel Red Hunter as well as Triumph's first parallel twin, the 6/1. Alongside this Page also designed a series of singles. However, the range was either too expensive for the common user, or the styling staid and uninspiring.

A lineage of speed. The Turner-designed Speed Twin (left) and the Page-designed 6/1 were pioneers of a new age of motorcycling cut short by the Second World War. But their legacy lived on in the 3HW. (Simon Davis)

A late war (1945) 3HW gleaming in RAF colours. Note the mudguard number plates, eschewed by Army dispatch riders, and the chrome exhaust. (Tony Hisgett)

By 1936 Page had moved on to BSA and was replaced as chief designer by the innovative Edward Turner who also fulfilled the role of general manager for the reborn Triumph brand. Among Turner's first tasks was the revitalization and simplification of the Triumph line-up that he had inherited from Page, this included the introduction of the new three-model Tiger range, the 70, 80 and 90. These were constructed around a single-tube frame, with engines featuring enclosed valve gear, stylish upswept exhausts, polished cases, all-important new finishes and wonderful chrome petrol tanks. They looked fast standing still and gave the owner an elegance hitherto restricted to the higher-end offerings.

In addition to the three Tigers there were three similar models of the same engine capacity, but with lower compressions and a more basic appearance, designated 2H, 3H and 5H, indicating engine capacity and overhead valves. These machines were intended to be used as everyday cheaper bikes. It was the 3H that would go on to form the basis of the military 3HW. Despite being cheaper, the 'H' range were still referred to as being 'de luxe' and featured chrome petrol tanks with gold-lined plum-coloured side panels.

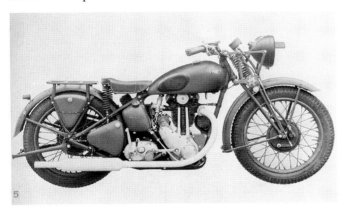

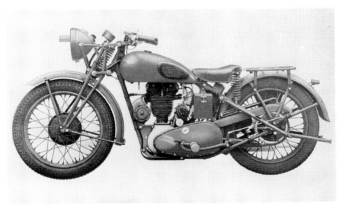

These wartime profile photos show an early 3HW which was little more than a matt green-painted Tiger 80 with a few additions. Some details, including the pannier-mounted storage box, didn't make it into production. (IWM)

All had four-speed, foot-change gearboxes along with electric lighting systems as standard, though a rear brake light remained an optional extra, along with an alternative engine sprocket for the 5H model to enable the attachment of sidecar. The Triumph range were now at the pinnacle of their game, providing motorcycles that featured great performance and handling allied with reliability and head-turning contemporary styling.

After an air raid by the Luftwaffe on 14 November 1940 destroyed the original Triumph Holbrook Lane works in Coventry, the 3HW was produced at an old foundry works in

The fuel tank-mounted Volkes dust filter, seen fitted to a Matchless G3/L, was a great aid in desert and dry environments where road dust was a problem. The 3HW featured a cutaway in the tail of the fuel tank to allow the clean air hose to pass into the carburettor mouth unhindered. (IWM)

Warwick from 1941 on using salvaged equipment and plant. The key difference between the civilian 3H and the military 3HW was the single-piece cast rocker box, which was now part of the cylinder head. Other key features included canvas saddlebags to the rear and the all-important headlight cover. Over 40,000 3HWs were produced during the war seeing service in all theatres.

A somewhat serious-looking Military Policeman in training at Mytchett near Aldershot, 31 March 1942. (IWM)

During the advance to Arnhem the Triumph was used by various units, including an attached rider from the Netherlands Brigade who arrived at the newly-liberated town of Eindhoven. The poor rider was mobbed by a crowd, and forced to endure a welcoming Bols or two from his ecstatic countryman and women. After half an hour he was seen by astounded members of the Irish Guards Group wobbling off into the distance carrying three children on his pillion seat and covered in orange blossom.

No matter how well trained you are or how good your kit is, sometimes you need a little help, provided in this instance by a Dutch child, to get out of a rut. (IWM)

Two MPs demonstrating a rudimentary wire cutter mounted to the forks. This was a real danger and many a dispatch rider was caught unawares by wire traps strung across roads, with often gruesome results. (IWM)

Elsewhere two members of the 90th City of London Field Regiment Royal Artillery had a lucky escape as they rode ahead of the main force on a reconnaissance mission. Their motorcycle was ambushed by a lone German soldier determined to stop them. Swerving to avoid the danger, the two men, Battery Sergeant Major Wilson and Lance Sergeant Krelle, went off the road, and immediately into the arms of a startled party of German infantry. Ditching the damaged motorbike, the two men miraculously avoided capture or worse by running back to the safety of their battery.

Boy and their Toys. Squadron Leader Johannes le Roux, DFC, Officer Commanding No. 111 Squadron, RAF, posing in front of his 3HW at 'Waterloo', a temporary airfield near Souk el Khemis, Tunisia, in 1943. Le Roux would later be responsible for the injury which incapacitated Rommel in 1944. (IWM)

Triumph 3HW Specifications:

Type: Lightweight single-cylinder motorcycle
Crew: 1 + 1 passenger
Wheelbase length: 1.3m
Total length: 2.1m
Front suspension: Web girder forks
Rear suspension: Rigid
Fuel tank: 14 litres
Engine: Triumph single-cylinder, 349cc, 4-speed, single-port OHV engine with automatic lubrication to rockers and valve guides (4F)
Performance:
    Engine: 20bhp
    Speed: 110kph
    Maximum range: 165km

CAMOUFLAGE AND MARKINGS

43rd Divisional Signals, Eindhoven, Netherlands, 19 September 1944. Divisional Signals provided signals and communications services purely for the division to which they were attached. This 3HW features all the usual refinements expected to be seen on a dispatch rider's mount. The fuel tank mounts the familiar blue-on-white tactical flash of the Royal Corps of Signals (RSigs) which remains in use today. This flash was only fitted to the port side (UK near side) of the fuel tank.

Among the many motorcycles available to the military the Triumph was the one that stood out, not least because the marque was synonymous with affordable speed, grace and quality before the war. So the opportunity to ride one must have been seized upon with relish. All Triumphs left the factories in either Desert Sand or shades of Olive Green before arriving

HQ Squadron, 2nd Armoured Battalion Grenadier Guards, 5th Guards Armoured Brigade, Guards Armoured Division, Schaft, 17 September 1944. Much like the Royal Corps of Signals, most larger units from battalion/regiment upwards maintained a pool of motorcycles for liaison use and the Guards Armoured Division were no exception. The familiar 'eye' insignia of the Guards Armoured Division rests on the front mudguard whilst the Triumph logo has been painted over, but remains visible just behind the registration number. Motorcycles such as this would have raced up and down the armoured columns of the Guards Armoured Division delivering important messages. Divisional motorcycles were often carried into battle on the back of armoured vehicles, being lowered when required to carry out liaison duties.

at parent units. Some were even given the tank Triumph logo, which was soon painted over. At this point in the war the front mudguard number plate had been removed and the registration number moved to both sides of the fuel tank.

QUARTERMASTER'S STORES

The Triumph 3HW has been covered by several manufacturers over the years, with the most notable kit being the 1/9 scale 1972 Esci model kit which has been released by various manufactures since 1972. In its latest incarnation the 3HW is offered by Italeri (Nr. 7402) with a range of markings that can be used to represent several units involved including Royal Signals troops. The kit has aged well, but the moulds are now beginning to look tired with seams present throughout, though a little fettling produces a fine model. Do study the instructions closely and compare to detail photographs as there are one or two anomalies.

Italeri's striking box art really helps sell its reboxed Esci 1/9 scale Triumph 3HW (Nr. 7402).

Due to the nature of the subject the kit is complex, and is best approached with patience. It really is one for the experienced modeller, or one who knows their way around a motorcycle. The vinyl pieces are nicely detailed, though the chain is extremely delicate and would have been better made from plastic. This

The decals are sharp and in register, with the whites being exceptionally brilliant. The mouldings are showing their age with seam lines aplenty but these are easily dealt with by the use of a sharp knife.

also sits between the rear wheel cogs as opposed to on top of them. Sadly there's no way around this strange arrangement. The build is best separated into stages for ease of painting and the lengths of fine tube used for control wiring are best added post construction. Overall the kit is a fine representation, and makes a handsome model once completed.

For the smaller scale modeller Bronco's 1/35 Triumph kit (Nr. CB35035) delivers three figures, photo-etch spokes, saddlebag straps and chain among other elements and enough plastic parts for two motorcycles. Like its 1/9 scale bedfellow this kit requires patience as it features numerous small parts, but makes up into wonderful little model, and with the three figures and two marking options, this kit really is a diorama in a box.

One way around the vinyl chain is the MFH resin and photo-etch chain set (Nr. 50288).

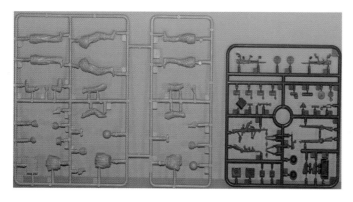

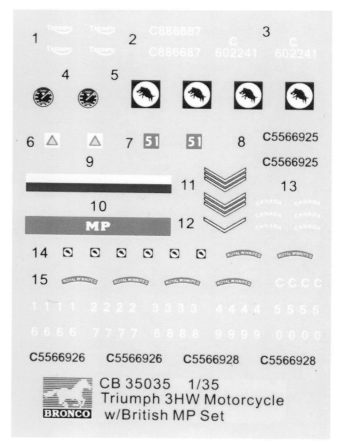

Bronco's 'diorama in a box' features some wonderfully-sculpted figures to go with the two 3HWs as well as some great photo-etch and decals, which includes rank chevrons and a host of registration numbers.

Other manufacturers include the South Korean resin company SOL, who supply their 3HW with photo-etch spokes, chain drive and details. Although a reasonable kit, it does look a little elongated and lacks some of the finesse of the Bronco kit.

South Korean 3D-printed model producers H3 Models have created a veritable work of art with their two-part 3HW. The benefits of 3D printing continue to grow for the modeller

and in the realm of smaller scale motorcycle modelling this production format will be king, with its ability to capture fine details. The appearance is spot on and the inclusion of the numerous cables and wires is testimony to the flexibility of 3D printing.

SHOWCASE BUILD
Italeri 1/9 Triumph 3HW, Dispatch Rider Mount, Guards Armoured Divisional Signals, Royal Corps of Signals. Ben Skipper

This Italeri kit is certainly not one for the faint-hearted, but with time and patience it can produce a lovely looking model. Originally released by ESCI in 1972 this kit has remained unchanged in the intervening 50 years. Coming with a range of markings options, I chose the Divisional Signals version as these would be the riders whose task would be to dash up and down the lines of static armour carrying important messages.

No aftermarket kits were used as, to be fair, there's only one, a chain set, to replace the vinyl band chain, which was unavailable at the time I made the kit, but the details are enough to produce a more-than-decent model. The build was straightforward and I followed the instructions to the number so to speak, leaving the exhaust, handlebars, saddlebags and vinyl piping off until the main body was painted.

The whole kit was primed in matt black before receiving a coat of Vallejo Bronze Green (71.250) with highlights made from

mixing Bronze Green and German Cam Beige (70.821). The engine and details were painted using a mix of Tamiya, Citadel and Vallejo colours with the tyres receiving a special Tamiya NATO Black (XF69) and Dark Sea Grey (XF 54) mix with ground brown pastel brushed over the tyres' surface once the paint had been left for 24 hours.

The next stage was to add the vinyl cables, which went on surprisingly easily, with the engine cables threaded under the fuel tank or alongside the engine block much like a real motorcycle. The final stage was to add the exhaust, handlebars and saddlebags and then give the model a gloss varnish before adding decals. This was followed by a light coat of thinned-down German Cam Beige and matt varnished mixed together to simulate the inevitable road dust that the bike would have accumulated on its journeys.

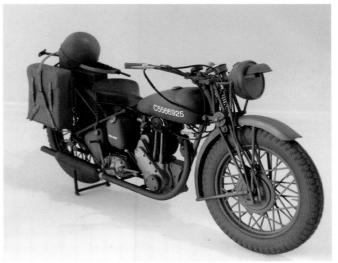
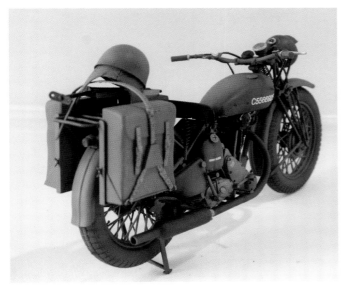

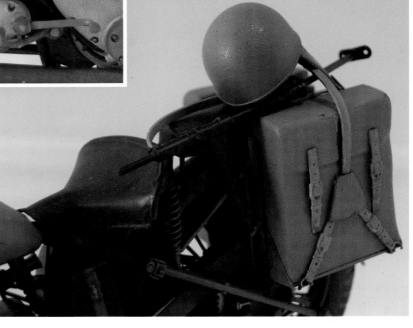